BETTER WRITING
From Paragraph to Essay

BETTER WRITING

From Paragraph to Essay

GENE STANFORD / MARIE N. SMITH

new york   chicago   san francisco   atlanta   dallas
montreal   toronto   london   sydney

holt, rinehart and winston

Library of Congress Cataloging in Publication Data

Stanford, Gene.
  Better writing.

  1. English language—Rhetoric. I. Smith,
Marie N., date, joint author. II. Title.
PE1408.S67   808'.042   80-142

ISBN 0-03-051161-5

0 1 2 3   059 9 8 7 6 5 4 3 2 1

To the Instructor

As any composition instructor knows, most texts are not really very helpful in teaching average students how to write. They neither present the basic principles of composition in a manner students can readily comprehend, nor do they allow students to build their knowledge step-by-step—grounding new principles in what they have already learned.

Many texts assume that students already know intuitively how to apply such complex concepts as *unit* and *development* or how to differentiate between *specific* and *general* in a writing situation. While they often flood students with pages of detailed discussions on *how* to write, they rarely require students to do much practice on their own. Moreover, most composition texts demonstrate the principles of composition with polished literary models from magazines and books—examples which may represent the acme of expository writing, but which many students cannot even follow, let alone appreciate and emulate. Such texts—years behind their equivalents in math and science—apparently assume that students will simply absorb these explanations and examples and then magically apply them when they finally sit down to write their own paragraphs or essays.

Such failings in most texts are significant, but the good instructor can overcome them in one way or another. There is one shortcoming that is more difficult to handle: the requirement that the instructor introduce, explain, and supervise nearly every step of the learning process. With more and more colleges giving students the opportunity to work independently in writing centers and laboratories, and with the staggering work load composition instructors currently have to carry, a self-teaching, self-checking text is desperately needed.

This book attempts to fill that need. Thirty-nine sections break down the skills of composition into small steps. Each step includes all the instructions students need in order to do their own work, as well as an Answer Key that allows them to check their answers. Hence, students can move at their own rates, practicing each skills, checking their achievement, and determining for themselves if they are ready to proceed. In order to give students opportunities to create wholly original compositions—and to double-check their progress from time to time—some exercises call for complete paragraphs and essays to be graded by the instructor (Steps 26, 32, 38, and 39, for example). But, in general, left alone with the book, students teach themselves, and the exercises need not be graded.

Because the instructor does not need to explain each new step or give all the instructions or check every exercise, a great deal of flexibility in the use of this book is possible. In a writing laboratory or writing workshop, where individual students work at their own paces, *Better Writing: from Paragraph to Essay* is ideally suited to individualized instruction. Students who need a basic introduction to paragraph and essay construction can be assigned to work through the entire book sequentially on their own. Other students who need only remedial help with specific skills can be referred to the sections of *Better Writing* that address their particular needs.

Even in the more conventional classroom format, in which a group of twenty to thirty students meets with an instructor for an hour three times a week, *Better Writing* is no less appropriate. The exercises may be completed during the class period—with students working individually while the instructor confers with students who need extra help, or with the total class working the exercises orally as a group, led by the teacher, or with students working in pairs to check each other's work. Or, alternately, the exercises can be assigned for out-of-class homework and then reviewed at the next class meeting, with the instructor providing further explanation of any skills that students find difficult.

• • •

Better Writing: from Paragraph to Essay is a revised and expanded version of an earlier work by one of the authors, *Steps to Better Writing* (Holt, 1972), which relied heavily on student writing for examples and exercises. Although not all of their contributions were used in the present volume, the following students again merit acknowledgement for their generosity in permitting adaptation and publication of their work: Keiley Caster, Richard Weston, Mark Rosenberg, Michael McDowell, Debbie McBride, Jack Whittier, Diane Jaworski, Charles Preston Seiss III, Randy Moresi, Barbara Shapiro, Ricky Shaikewitz, Jack Engler,

Bruce Fonarow, Steve Block, Susan Chen, Robert Soell, John Stokes, Howard Mirowitz, Helane Wilen, Jeff Osman, June Westerhold, Mark Pasek, Janet Nebel, Wes Burgess, Sharon Pearline, Edward Thoenes, John Richardson, Marsha Sherman, Ellen Cohen, Lori Glassman, Lindy Gredizer, Mara Goldfarb, Linda Rich, and Booker Green.

We are also grateful to the following, who read the manuscript and made valuable suggestions: R.S. Beal, Boston University, Sandra Kornbar, Glassboro State College, David Martin, Monmouth College, Dr. Shirley Morahan, Northeast Missouri State University, Michael Policastro, Ramapo College, David Skwire, Cuyahoga Community College, Bonnie Stevens, College of Wooster.

G.S.
M.N.S.

To the Student

This workbook is based on a simple premise: that writing, like playing the guitar or winning at tennis, is the result of a series of easily identifiable skills. No one of these skills is, by itself, difficult to master, but each one is essential to the writing process. The format of the book introduces you to each skill, each step in the process of writing well, in turn. The skill will be explicitly identified and explained, and a variety of tasks and exercises will be provided to enable you to understand and practice the skill involved.

Each skill builds on the skills learned previously, so that you will accumulate a wide range of writing resources to draw on whenever you face a writing situation. First, you will develop an understanding of expository writing as the combination of two basic human behaviors: generalizing and specifying. Then you will learn to develop a restricted topic into a paragraph by a formula which can apply to any paragraph you will ever need to write. Another skill you will learn is developing in detail rather than simply listing the statements that support your topic sentence, and you will learn to put your supporting statements in the most appealing and convincing order. Your writing will become more fluent and coherent as you practice techniques for weaving your sentences together and filling the gaps in your thinking.

Having mastered paragraph construction, you will proceed to longer compositions, and you will discover that an essay, while being made up of paragraphs, is also simply an enlargement of a paragraph, and thus capitalizes on many of the same skills you learned previously. You will receive guidance in writing three complete essays and, finally, will practice revising and evaluating your own work.

The intention of this book is to give you the basic tools needed by any writer, not to turn you into a Hemingway or a Shakespeare. Only a few talented people can become literary artists, but all students can learn to express themselves coherently and effectively if they are aware of every step of the writing process and have a basic writing formula which they can apply to a multitude of writing situations.

Reducing writing to a simple formula may strike you as rather rigid and limiting. It certainly would be if you never moved beyond it. Once you have mastered it, you will most surely wish to experiment with variations and alter the principles in this book to fit the unique requirements of each writing situation you encounter.

If you faithfully follow each step in this book, you will achieve competence in the use of the basic tools of writing and will then be able to develop your own writing style with greater confidence and success.

Contents

BETTER WRITING
From Paragraph to Essay

Distinguishing between Specific and General I

STEP 1	Understanding Specific and General

The primary obligation of writers of exposition is to develop in detail each generalization they introduce. This obligation entails, at the very least, a need to restate general words, phrases, or sentences in more specific language. At the most, it can entail the production of chapter after chapter of explanation, illustration, and proof of an intricate and profound idea which is the subject of a book.

Students sometimes protest, "But why do I need all those extra words? I've said it once. Isn't that enough?"

The answer is, quite simply, *no*. That is not enough. Specification of a general statement is *not* padding. If people were easily informed, convinced, taught or beguiled by bare one-sentence statements of general ideas, there would be no books or essays. We would merely pass around outlines showing the general framework of our thinking. Gone would be explanations, case histories, illustrations, descriptions, supporting data, authoritative quotations, logical arguments, and all the other details of which books, essays, and even ordinary paragraphs are composed. Gone, in short, would be writing.

For the writer, the category of *General* includes statements of ideas (generalizations), and the category of *Specific* includes all the writing

1

required to present the idea in detail (specification). Writers must be able to work consciously within each category, and they must always know the difference between them. They must also recognize that these terms are relative and that a word may be general in one context and specific in another. The exercises that follow will reinforce your understanding of the relationship between these two terms.

• EXERCISE

Label each of the words, phrases, or statements in each pair below S for specific or G for general. Remember that a specific word or statement refers to a part of a whole or one member of a class or group. A general word or statement refers to a whole thing or a class or group of things. Example:

  _S_ basketball   _G_ sports

1. ——— novel

   ——— *Gone with the Wind*

2. ——— building

   ——— shed

3. ——— Los Angeles

   ——— city

4. ——— clothing

   ——— shirt

5. ——— school subjects

   ——— mathematics

6. ——— learning to hold the racket

   ——— learning to play tennis

7. ——— my messy room

   ——— clothes all over the floor

8. ——— installing a C.B. radio in my car

   ——— drilling a hole for the antenna cable

9. ——— attempting to be courteous

   ——— holding the door open for someone

10. ——— carefully measuring one cup of sugar

——— making cookies on a Saturday afternoon

11. ——— Mr. Robertson is a good citizen.

——— Mr. Robertson votes in every election.

12. ——— There's nothing more exciting than spending the day at an amusement park.

——— Some people are afraid to ride the Ferris wheel.

13. ——— Drag racing can be dangerous.

——— Many people have been killed in drag races.

14. ——— Punishment is sometimes used to make rebellious children obey their parents.

——— My father used a belt to whip me when I was a child.

15. ——— Bob Dixon is our team's best basketball player.

——— Bob Dixon scored all thirty-six of our team's points in last night's game.

16. ——— An accomplished chef is able to produce dishes from the cuisine of any nationality.

——— Pierre Annaud is French, but he makes magnificent lasagna.

17. ——— Walt Whitman was roundly condemned for his use of free verse.

——— Any artist who introduces a radically new and different art form will suffer much criticism.

Check your answers on p. 169 before continuing.

STEP 2

Relating Specific and General

A word or statement is never always specific or always general. To determine whether it is specific or general one must look at what other word or statement it is compared to. For example "tree" is *general* when compared to "oak," since "tree" is the group or class to which "oak" belongs. But "tree" is *specific* when compared to "plant" since "tree" is only one member among many in the class "plant."

• EXERCISE

Number the items in each list below in order of increasing specificity. Place a 1 beside the most general term, a 2 beside the term which is somewhat more specific, a 3 beside the term which is even more specific, and so on.

1. ——— planet

   ——— house

   ——— street

   ——— state

   ——— nation

   ——— city

2. ——— Tim

   ——— male

   ——— animal

   ——— human being

   ——— boy

3. ——— developing a broader world perspective

   ——— learning a foreign language

   ——— meeting people from different cultures

   ——— exposing oneself to differing viewpoints

   ——— reading periodicals in another language

4. ——— I try to run at least three miles each day.

   ——— While running last night, I was almost struck by a careless driver.

   ——— Regular exercise is essential for good health.

   ——— Aerobic exercise improves the body's cardiovascular system.

   ——— Jogging and swimming are excellent aerobic activities.

5. ——— One should not become totally immersed in one's job.

   ——— My church sponsors a weekly dinner-dance.

   ——— One's social life should be entirely separated from one's work.

   ——— Last Saturday night French cuisine and music were featured.

   ——— My social life centers around my church.

6. _____ Many people are no longer able to afford meat.

_____ Inflation steals the rewards of hard work.

_____ Food prices have risen steadily for years.

_____ Even a generous pay raise is offset by rising prices.

_____ Inflation is our silent enemy.

7. _____ I prefer traveling by automobile to any other form of travel.

_____ My family has always owned Chevrolet cars, which are very comfortable on long trips.

_____ I feel that American cars are designed better for travel than are foreign cars.

_____ My favorite pastime is traveling.

_____ We now have a bright red Chevrolet—just in time for a trip to Walt Disney World.

8. _____ Slaves were generally sold at auctions, in the same manner as cattle or hogs.

_____ Most historians believe that there were many reasons for the Civil War.

_____ Often a good slave would sell for as much as fifteen hundred dollars.

_____ One reason for the Civil War was the South's refusal to abolish the lucrative practice of black slavery.

_____ The Civil War was an important historical event in America.

Check your answers on p. 169 before continuing.

STEP 3   Adding Up Specifics

When a number of specifics are "added together," we can label the group with a general term. For example, if we add together Bill, Tom, John, Sam, Mike and Bob, we get the general term *boy*. Of if we add together Ford, Plymouth, Chevrolet, Buick and Datsun, we come up with the general term *automobile*. Another way of arriving at a generalization is to ask, "What do all of these terms have in common? Is there perhaps a special way in which they are related?" Fords, Plymouths, Chevrolets, Buicks and Datsuns have in common the fact that they are all automobiles, and so the general term is *automobile*. (A group of specifics may be related in more than one way, such as in the case of the first example above, where the general term *first name* may be substituted for *boy*.)

• EXERCISE A

Circle the letter of the item in each group below that is general enough to include or summarize all the other items.

1. a) sofa
   b) chair
   c) bed
   d) table
   e) stool
   f) furniture

2. a) oak
   b) elm
   c) pine
   d) tree
   e) hickory
   f) maple

3. a) diagramming sentences
   b) studying English
   c) making book reports
   d) reading short stories
   e) writing paragraphs
   f) learning grammar rules

4. a) taking a shower
   b) shining your shoes
   c) getting ready for an important date
   d) combing your hair
   e) making sure your best suit is pressed
   f) shaving

5. a) It is easier to park.
   b) It usually requires less gas.
   c) Repair bills are generally lower.
   d) A small car has many advantages over a large one.
   e) License tags are less expensive.

6. a) The new Lincoln Center was a brilliant success in its first season.
   b) The choreographer breathed new life into the classical ballet.
   c) A variety of entertainment was presented all winter.
   d) The performance of "Swan Lake" was hailed by audience and critics alike.
   e) The New York City Ballet Company performed throughout January.

7. a) Hot soup warms you all over.
   b) Even dieters can eat soup without feeling guilty.
   c) All children seem to love bean soup.
   d) Meat or chicken adds extra nutrition to any soup.
   e) A good nourishing soup is hard to beat.

8. a) Making mistakes keeps one from becoming self-righteous.
   b) Good health is as much a product of the mind as of the body.
   c) One cannot always count on people behaving as one would prefer.
   d) If we live long enough, life teaches us many lessons we need to learn.
   e) Years of painful practice improve one's ability to admit error.

9. a) The British Hovercraft Corporation has planned a transoceanic vessel that would carry 140 passengers; a freighter hovercraft is also foreseeable.
   b) Hovercraft—vehicles that ride on a cushion of air produced by downward pointed fans and are driven by propellers—have many intriguing possibilities for the future of transportation.
   c) Hovertrains would apply the hovercraft principle to overland travel, operating on concrete thoroughfares at speeds up to 250 miles per hour.
   d) Because hovercraft are immune to sonar and torpedoes, they are particularly attractive to the military—especially the Navy and Coast Guard.
   e) The perfect vessel for a ferry seems to be a hovercraft because its wide, low construction offers plenty of space for automobiles.

10. a) Television broadcasters even control some of the rules under which athletic events are played.
    b) The starting time of a game is often delayed or changed to another date to suit the convenience of the television networks.
    c) Telecast games must also be stopped frequently for commercials.
    d) Television is exercising too much control over athletic events.

11. a) A stream of grapejuice is oozing from the crack in the refrigerator door.
    b) A two-year-old boy and his security blanket have just plundered the kitchen.

    c) One third of tonight's dinner has been dragged from the counter to the floor.

    d) Unlaced, lying on the table, is an unmated left shoe.

    e) A heap of nursery rhyme books is flung over a pile of newspapers.

    f) Mother is standing exasperated in the doorway.

12. a) Detours are seldom as clearly marked as a driver would like.

    b) The scenery one has looked forward to enjoying is blocked by earth moving equipment and mounds of dirt and gravel.

    c) Dust hangs in the air and chokes one's breathing.

    d) Traveling through extensive road construction is far from enjoyable.

    e) It is disappointing to be able to travel only half as many miles as one had planned.

13. a) A pair of high-topped boots provides needed ankle support.

    b) Proper equipment is important to a good target shooter.

    c) A sling supports the gun and relaxes the tension on arm muscles, thus preventing fatigue.

    d) The shooter's glove is generally made of very soft leather and resembles a knight's gauntlet with the ends of the fingers cut off.

    e) A special jacket with a leather pad near the shoulder helps to keep the butt of the gun from slipping.

    f) Perhaps the most important piece of equipment is a custom fitted gun.

Check your answers on p. 169 before continuing.

• EXERCISE B

In the space provided under each list of specifics below, write a general term (word, phrase, or sentence) which summarizes the list. It may be helpful for you to visualize each list as an addition problem to which you are to supply the answer by "adding up" the specifics. In some instances, more than one answer is possible, but choose only one.

1. boat
    train
    plane
    car
    bus

    General Statement _____

2. dogs
   cats
   rabbits
   goldfish
   parakeets

   GS _____

3. French
   English
   Spanish
   Japanese
   Italian

   GS _____

4. listing all negative arguments one can think of
   listing all affirmative arguments one can think of
   carefully examining one's feelings
   anticipating views and reactions of all people involved
   getting advice from experienced and well informed people

   GS _____

5. finding a quiet place, away from distractions
   making sure that I have enough light
   gathering all the books, materials, and equipment that I need
   checking that there is plenty of fresh air

   GS _____

6. scanning the lines
   identifying the meter
   checking the rhyme scheme
   looking for allusions
   identifying metaphorical language
   observing the connotations of words

   GS _____

7. Typing is one of the fastest, neatest, and most efficient methods of
   writing available to the student.
   Typing consumes less space on the paper than script, enabling the
   writer to include more ideas on a page.
   This mode of writing presents an ideal opportunity for the student to
   make better grades, since all teachers like easy-to-read typewritten
   work.

Since typing is one of the standard requirements for clerical work, this skill qualifies one for a good summer job.

GS _____

8. My driving instructor is biting his nails.
   With breath held, he covers his face with his hands.
   He retightens his seat belt.
   His foot hovers unsteadily over the safety brake.

   GS _____

9. Sen. Robert Taft, son of William Howard Taft, twenty-seventh President of the United States, was never quite able to get the Republican nomination for the Presidency.
   After retiring from the army, John Eisenhower became Ambassador to Belgium.
   One or another of the Crosby sons is frequently seen on television.
   Winston Churchill's son was a journalist.
   Theodore Roosevelt, Jr. was an officer in the U. S. Army.

   GS _____

10. Chad could usually expend a full ten minutes sharpening several pencils.
    He would lay out paper in a neat stack on the desk.
    Finding a dictionary was never easy, but he refused to start work before he had one at hand.
    Then the search for the thesaurus began.
    Finally, he would have another cup of coffee to fortify himself for the ordeal ahead.

    GS _____

Check the Answer Key on p. 170 before continuing.

STEP 4   Perceiving Relationships

• EXERCISE

For each pair of charts below, a list of items has been provided. In the spaces on the charts write the letters of the items which would properly fit there. Note that one item has already been placed on each chart to give you a hint. This exercise should be a reminder to you that a word (the one given) can be either specific or general, depending on what other word it is compared to.

1. a) transportation
    b) Plymouth
    c) train
    d) plane
    e) Ford
    f) Chevrolet
    g) Dodge
    h) bus

SP _____   SP _____

SP _____   SP _____

SP _____   SP _____

SP _____   SP car

*GS car   GS _____

2. a) daisy
    b) tree
    c) plant
    d) rose
    e) bush
    f) violet
    g) grass
    h) marigold

SP _____   SP _____

SP _____   SP _____

SP _____   SP _____

SP _____   SP flower

GS flower   GS _____

3. a) visiting the Capitol
    b) sightseeing in New York

---

* Throughout this book, SP refers to a specific word or statement; GS refers to a general word or statement

c) spending hours trudging through the Smithsonian Institution
d) traveling through the Midwest
e) touring the United States
f) sightseeing up-hill-and-down in San Francisco
g) walking leisurely under the cherry trees near the Lincoln Memorial
h) touring the White House

SP _____   SP _____

SP _____   SP _____

SP _____   SP _____

SP _____   SP visiting Washington, D.C.

GS visiting Washington, D.C.   GS _____

4. a) The power loom helped to increase the amount of cloth which could
       be produced each year.
    b) The steam engine provided an efficient, inexpensive means for trans-
       porting goods.
    c) Improvements in agricultural methods made possible the support of
       large urban populations needed to run factories.
    d) The spinning jenny produced thread faster and more efficiently than
       the hand operated wheel.
    e) Discovery of new uses for natural resources was a contributing factor.
    f) Standardized parts helped make mass production possible.
    g) The water wheel introduced a new source of power.
    h) The Industrial Revolution was the result of many events and develop-
       ments.

SP _____   SP _____

SP _____   SP _____

SP _____   SP _____

SP _____   SP The invention of many important

GS The invention of many impor-   machines helped to produce the
    tant machines helped to pro-   Industrial Revolution
    duce the Industrial Revolution   GS _____

Check your answers on p. 170 before continuing.

STEP 5   **Supplying Specifics**

• EXERCISE

Supply specific words, phrases or sentences that could logically be summarized by the general word, phrase, or sentence provided in each of the charts below. In other words, list items that "add up" to the "total" that is given.

1. SP _____

    SP _____

    SP _____

    SP _____

    GS toys

2. SP _____

    SP _____

    SP _____

    SP _____

    GS sports

3. SP _____

    SP _____

    SP _____

    SP _____

    GS washing the car

4. SP _____

    SP _____

    SP _____

    SP _____

    GS preparing for a trip to the beach

5. SP _____

   SP _____

   SP _____

   SP _____

   GS reading the newspaper

6. SP _____

   SP _____

   SP _____

   SP _____

   GS The automobile influences our lives in many ways.

7. SP _____

   SP _____

   SP _____

   SP _____

   GS Good teachers have certain characteristics.

Check the Answer Key on p. 170 before continuing.

STEP 6   Finding the General Statement

• EXERCISE

In the exercise below, groups of sentences have been put together, sometimes in proper order, sometimes in scrambled order. In each group, underline the one sentence that is general enough to summarize or include all the others.

1. Many elderly people are forced to live alone, with little contact with others. Country people who move to the city feel friendless and uprooted. In the large cities people are seldom acquainted with their neighbors. Poverty prevents many people from going places where they can form friendly associations. Even in the midst of crowds of people, many are lonely. People who have no family are forced to turn to social agencies when they are in need.

2. We spent hours trudging through the Smithsonian Institution, but the exhibits were interesting and worth the effort. The weather was warm, and we enjoyed walking leisurely under the cherry trees near the Lincoln Memorial. Our trip to Washington, D.C. was the high point of the summer. We took a tour of the White House and even caught sight of the President as he came out the front door. My uncle, who works in the Pentagon, showed us through that huge building. I'll bet we walked twenty miles through the long corridors.

3. Young people derive their morals from many sources. Of course parents and home life have the greatest influence, for young people tend to pattern their behavior after that of their first examples. But they soon begin to recognize that some of their friends from different backgrounds hold moral standards at variance with their own, and they are affected by these differences. Soon young people begin to develop their own moral codes, influenced by standards expressed in newspapers, books, magazines, radio, television, movies, and by adults in the community. Religion may also influence the development of young people's moral beliefs. In many cases, however, organized religion has not met this challenge and has presented youth with guidance which is either too outdated or too hypocritical to have any relevance to their lives.

4. Using a mass transit system would cost passengers less than driving their own cars by saving them the price of gas, automobile maintenance, and parking fees. A well-planned mass transit network offers many advantages to a city and its citizens. Mass transit offers an attractive alternative to the building of more highways in the city, a move which would perhaps lessen burdensome taxes for highway construction and would take up little space in comparison to the highway "jungle." Also, the need for huge parking facilities would be eliminated from city plans, because most people could simply walk from the mass transit station to their work. In addition, the system would be a source of income for the city as well as for the company operating it. Finally, if the system were well organized, travelers could avoid the long drive to and from the airport and other distant facilities.

5. Since the alligator is an amphibious creature, it needs a place to swim. The best place to keep such a pet is in a fenced in pond or small lake. If a pond is not available, a large metal swimming pool will do, provided that the water does not contain large amounts of chemicals. Whether the alligator is kept in a pond or in a pool, there should always be abundant vegetation surrounding the area. Although the alligator is not a herbivorous animal, it needs this heavy vegetation as a source of camouflage and protection from the sun. The alligator is a cold-blooded animal; it cannot regulate its body temperature. Therefore, the temperature of the area surrounding it must be kept well above freezing or the reptile will die. An

alligator must have a natural-like environment in order to survive in captivity.

6. When animals are sleepy, they find a quiet place and go to sleep. Human beings, on the other hand, often force themselves to stay awake and suffer afterwards from lack of sufficient rest. The instincts of animals seem to enable them to preserve their health more efficiently than does the vaunted intelligence of human beings. Animals eat what is good for them in quantities that satisfy the needs of their bodies. The eating habits of many people, when they have a choice of food, are unwise and conducive to numerous bodily ailments. Many people drive themselves to a frantic level of activity that causes stress far beyond what their bodies can safely endure. Animals exercise until they are tired, then stop and rest. Human beings often demonstrate a perverse desire to engage in dangerous activities, sometimes as a test of skill, at other times as a way of expressing their superiority over other persons. Animals almost always show more regard for their own safety. They avoid danger whenever possible.

7. One situation which can be very distressing to people is the occasional time when a friend, teacher, or relative loses faith in them. If they accidentally double-cross a friend, do not live up to a teacher's expectations, or do something that their parents feel is morally wrong, the feeling of utter failure which ensues can cause deep despondency. A second situation of this sort is one in which a best friend changes from someone who cares about everything and everyone into a snob and a social climber. It is totally disheartening to realize that a person once entirely worthy of confidence is now someone who is capable of ridiculing and snubbing others. Finally, there is the experience of performing badly, which everyone has been through. Whether it is losing a hockey game by making a stupid pass, giving a terrible speech, or not being able to memorize a musical piece perfectly, the feeling one gets of wanting to dig a hole and jump into it is almost worse than death. In short, though one cannot know what death is like, having never experienced it, some situations which arise in daily life seem as if they must surely be worse than dying.

Check your answers on p. 171 before continuing.

II
Composing the Basic Paragraph

Writing a Topic Sentence

• **EXERCISE**

When specific ideas and the general statement that summarizes them are arranged into a paragraph, the general statement is often called the "topic sentence" because it tells the reader what general topic the paragraph is about. In the paragraphs below the topic sentences have been omitted. In the blank provided write a topic sentence for each by composing a general statement that summarizes all the specific statements in each paragraph. Make sure your statement is a complete sentence (hint: do not begin it with "why" or "how"), and that it is general enough to incorporate all of the other sentences.

1. _____

_____

_____ . Proper feeding is as important to a lawn as it is to a household pet. Fertilizer, available at any hardware or discount store, should be applied three times during the growing season—early in the spring, in mid-summer, and late in the fall. Watering the lawn is also important, particularly in hot, dry climates. A thorough soaking

17

once each week will keep the grass green and healthy. And do not overlook the importance of cutting the lawn regularly at the proper height. No more than one inch should be clipped off each time the grass is cut; otherwise, damage to the grass plants can result.

2. _____

_____

_____ . First of all, attempt to become actively involved in the process. Think about the material being read and don't just plow through it as though repeating the Pledge to the Flag. A good practice is to skim over section headings in the assigned chapter before a more detailed reading. These headings do more than create a pleasing page appearance. They show how the author has organized ideas, and they clarify the major points. Reading chapter summaries is also a good way to preview chapters. The chapter headings and any introduction supplied by the teacher will often tend to raise questions in your mind about the material. Be aware of these and any other questions that arise during the reading and look for the answers. In addition, it is wise to take time out periodically from reading to recite to yourself the important points being learned. A quick quiz or review exercise, self-imposed, will help to fix ideas firmly in your mind. Finally, after reading the entire assignment, review the main points by looking over the chapter headings and skimming for the central ideas of the text.

3. _____

_____

_____ . The amateur photographer who can sell a photo to a magazine or newspaper will find that it is most lucrative. Often a publication will pay as much as $100 for a single photograph. The production of humorous or exciting pictures through the use of trick photography is another rewarding part of this hobby. While such pictures may not always sell readily, the amateur still has the satisfaction of having created something unusual. Photographs entered in a contest stand a chance of winning not only a monetary award, but also the accompanying recognition and prestige. Since photography is used both in the mass media and in the fields of science, medicine, and law, the young people who make photography a hobby are also preparing themselves for any number of interesting careers.

4. _____

_____

_____ . If some animals

were not killed by hunters, they would continue to multiply at a geometric rate, and nature would not be able to keep the species' numbers down. This surplus could cause millions of dollars worth of damage to farmers' crops and to the ecological balance in general. There would be so great a number of these animals that the likelihood of disease epidemics would increase. The result could be very serious health problems, not only for animals, but also for human beings. When animals are allowed to multiply in unrestricted numbers—especially now that so many natural predators have been eliminated—there is often not enough food to go around and they starve. Hunting these animals, therefore, is often more merciful than letting them meet a slow and painful death by starvation or disease.

Check the Answer Key on p. 171 before continuing.

<table>
<tr><td>STEP
8</td><td>**Eliminating
Unrelated Specifics**</td></tr>
</table>

A basic requirement for a developed paragraph in expository writing is that it adhere to the principle of *unity*. That is, it must be unified around the topic introduced in the topic sentence.

It is not enough, however, that the paragraph deal only with the topic—the subject—introduced. It must deal specifically with what the topic sentence says *about* the subject. For instance, if a topic sentence states that, "The dog is man's best friend," the paragraph that follows must be confined not only to the subject of dogs, but more specifically, to the fact that dogs are man's best friend. If the writer has other interesting comments to make about dogs, they must go into another paragraph with another topic sentence.

A given topic sentence may be developed (explained, clarified, proved, and so on) in more than one paragraph if the number of specific ideas becomes so extensive as to merit division into separate paragraphs for each of the specific aspects. The opposite is not true, however: if the specification of a general statement (a topic sentence) is very brief, the writer cannot for that or any other reason group several such general statements, along with their specification, in one paragraph.

Paragraph unity represents an inescapable agreement between writers and their readers: one topic idea to a paragraph, with every statement in the paragraph referring to that idea. The following exercise calls on you to apply the principle of unity.

• EXERCISE

Cross out the items in each list below that do not belong. That is, eliminate those that do not fall under the category given by the general term. Each list may contain more than one irrelevant term.

1. automobiles
    a) Cadillac
    b) Boeing 707
    c) Plymouth
    d) Ford
    e) Pontiac
    f) Greyhound

2. fish
    a) trout
    b) mackerel
    c) salmon
    d) seal
    e) tuna
    f) seagull

3. efficient study habits
    a) taking complete notes
    b) reading textbook assignments carefully
    c) forgetting important assignments by failing to write them down
    d) organizing study time
    e) choosing quiet surroundings with adequate lighting
    f) leaving all work until the last minute
    g) having necessary books and materials at hand to avoid wasting time looking for them
    h) reviewing class notes periodically

4. preparation for a trip to a foreign country
    a) One should make hotel reservations in advance.
    b) Some foreign countries are not safe for tourists if they leave the major cities.
    c) One should plan a wardrobe that is versatile and easy to carry.
    d) Most foreign countries have at least an American consul who can be helpful to travelers who have troubles.
    e) One should have an exact itinerary planned for the entire trip.
    f) It pays to learn some basic words or phrases in the language of the country being visited.
    g) One should behave in ways that reflect credit on the United States.

5. What a good pop music group should have
    a) It should have its own distinct "sound" and should not try to imitate other groups.
    b) It will be interesting to see whether punk rock has more than a brief vogue.
    c) A good group will get the audience involved in its music.
    d) One of the best features of many good bands is their ability to write their own music.
    e) A good manager is a definite asset to a band.
    f) Today's pop music groups, if they hit it big, can make a tremendous amount of money.

6. There are many things a careful driver does to reduce the possibility of an accident.
    a) One must be careful to dim the headlights whenever another car approaches.
    b) A good driver watches the road ahead very carefully, keeping alert for a situation that could lead to an accident, such as a car pulling onto the highway.
    c) To get a license, the driver must pass both a written and a driving test.
    d) One must make sure the automobile is in top operating condition.
    e) Speeding is sometimes necessary, as in the case of rushing an injured person to the hospital.
    f) A good driver obeys all traffic laws.
    g) Today's cars have too much horsepower to be safe.
    h) One must watch out for the mistakes of other drivers.

7. One cannot achieve peace of mind without first developing a capacity for self discipline.
    a) A person who routinely fails to live up to obligations is likely to feel guilty much of the time.
    b) Oversleeping in the morning often sets a frantic pace for the entire day.
    c) One who does the very best one can with every task has few regrets.
    d) A person who tries to be all things to all people tends to become hypocritical.
    e) To get enough sleep to feel rested throughout an active day, one often has to resist the temptation of late night TV programs.
    f) Peace of mind can also derive from one's religious beliefs or a philosophy of life that one has developed over the years.
    g) It is difficult to feel proud of oneself if one habitually avoids challenges to achieve at a high level.

Check your answers on p. 171 before continuing.

STEP 9   Supplying Specifics

• EXERCISE

Supply three or four specific statements which help to explain or prove each of the general statements below. Be sure that all specifics are directly related to the general statement in question.

1. GS The C.B. radio has dramatically changed the relationship between drivers on the highway.

      SP _____

      SP _____

      SP _____

      SP _____

2. GS Good parents always strive to be fair with their children.

      SP _____

      SP _____

      SP _____

      SP _____

3. GS Good drivers are made, not born.

      SP _____

      SP _____

      SP _____

      SP _____

4. GS Parents will find the years when their children are adolescents the most difficult to live through.

      SP _____

      SP _____

      SP _____

      SP _____

Check the Answer Key on p. 171 before continuing.

STEP 10

Arranging Items in Paragraph Form

The lists you made in Step 9 are simple paragraph outlines. To convert them into complete paragraphs, you use the general statement (GS) as the topic sentence and place it first in the paragraph, making sure to indent the first line about one-half inch from the left-hand margin. Following the topic sentence you present the supporting specifics (SP's) that you have listed, along with any additional information that is needed to explain the specifics.

When turning a list of specifics into a paragraph, you may discover that you need to insert connecting words or phrases between the specifics. These connectors, usually called transitional words, include expressions such as *also, next, on the other hand, finally, in addition,* and many others. Without them, a paragraph may not flow smoothly from one idea to another. Take, for example, the following paragraph diagram:

GS Diabetes causes much inconvenience in the life of a person who has it.
SP The person must inject insulin every day.
SP The person must carefully regulate food intake.
SP The person must regulate the amount of exercise he or she gets.

If the writer does not provide transitional words between the specifics when turning this diagram into a complete paragraph, the paragraph that results does not flow smoothly, even if the writer includes additional information to explain the specifics:

Diabetes causes much inconvenience in the life of a person who has it. The person must inject insulin every day, and this procedure requires testing of urine and keeping up with all the necessary equipment. The person must carefully regulate food intake, since the amount of sugar eaten must match the insulin dose. The diabetic must regulate the amount of exercise he or she gets. Regular exercise is essential, but too much can be harmful if the insulin dose is not adjusted accordingly.

Much of the awkwardness and choppiness of that paragraph can be eliminated by the addition of some simple transitional expressions:

Diabetes causes much inconvenience in the life of a person who has it. *For example*, the person must inject insulin every day, and this procedure requires testing of urine and keeping up with all the necessary equipment. *In addition*, the person must carefully regulate food intake, since the amount of sugar eaten must match the insulin dose. *As if that were not enough*, the diabetic must *also* regulate the amount of exercise he or she gets. Regular exercise is essential, but too much can be harmful if the insulin dose is not adjusted accordingly.

The use of connecting or transitional words will be discussed in more detail in Step 19. Meanwhile, when writing a paragraph, you should feel free to add transitional expressions when they make sense and help the reader follow the ideas.

• EXERCISE

Using one of the lists in Step 9, write a complete paragraph. Use the general statement as the topic sentence at the beginning of the paragraph, remembering to indent the first line about one-half inch from the left-hand margin. Support this sentence with the specific ideas you listed in Step 9, adding any other information and transitional expressions that you feel are needed. Write the paragraph in the space provided below.

_____

_____

_____

_____

_____

_____

_____

_____

_____

_____

_____

_____

_____

_____
_____
_____
_____
_____
_____
_____

Check the Answer Key on p. 172 before continuing.

<table>
<tr><td>

STEP
11

</td><td>

Listing Both
General Statement
and Supporting Specifics

</td></tr>
</table>

• EXERCISE

For three of the topics given below, write a general statement in your own words (as you did in Step 3, Exercise B, and in Step 7). Then list three or four supporting specific statements for each (as you did in Step 9). Make sure your general statement is a complete sentence. Do not simply copy the topic as it appears here. Check each list to be sure that all the specifics explain or prove the general statement. If there are some which do not, cross them out and add any others that occur to you.

a) My Favorite Pastime (Game, Hobby, Sport)
b) Why Reading Is Necessary
c) The Loss of a Friend
d) Being Fired from a Job
e) My Biggest Disappointment
f) Getting Along with Roommates

1. GS _____

_____

   SP _____

   SP _____

   SP _____

   SP _____

2. GS _____

 _____

   SP _____

   SP _____

   SP _____

   SP _____

3. GS _____

 _____

   SP _____

   SP _____

   SP _____

   SP _____

Check the Answer Key on p. 172 before continuing.

STEP 12 — Arranging Items in Paragraph Form

• EXERCISE

Turn one of your lists from Step 11 into a paragraph, using your general statement (GS) as the topic sentence and your list of specifics (SP's) to support it. Explain each specific statement with at least one additional sentence, adding any information that helps explain the specific idea. Write your paragraph in the space provided below, indent the first line of your paragraph about one-half inch from the left-hand margin, and keep your margins on both sides as straight as possible. Then underline the topic sentence and number the specifics in the order they appear in the paragraph, as shown in the following example.

A veritable paper revolution in the last fifty years has made life more convenient and pleasant in ways now taken quite for granted.[1] The linen handkerchief, once the pride of ladies and gentlemen alike, has long since given way, for the most part, to a rainbow array of tissues made to be used once and discarded. Few homemakers would care to go back to the days of laundering seven handkerchiefs a week for each family member.[2] Paper now makes homemaking vastly easier, especially in the kitchen. Paper towels and paper napkins have taken over almost universally from their cloth counterparts that used to add so much volume to the family wash, and all kinds of waxy papers for wrapping lunches and packaging leftover foods make food care a simple task.[3] In fact, packaging of food in some form of paper product has revolutionized the entire food processing and marketing industry. Milk bottles are a thing of the past, along with the barrels and bins and cloth bags which once held products in bulk at stores where people shopped.[4] Now, when people go shopping, they carry home an unbelievable assortment of boxes and bags inside their big paper shopping bags. Paper wrappers for bread, paperboxes for cookies, cartons for cheese, paper labels on cans and, finally, a paper tape to list all purchases—all are products of a paper explosion that has changed our way of life.

_____

_____

_____

_____

_____

_____

_____

_____

_____

_____

_____

_____

_____

_____

_____

_____

_____

_____

_____

_____

_____

_____

_____

After writing your paragraph, check the Answer Key
on p. 173 before continuing.

STEP 13   Extending Specifics

From the previous lessons, you have learned to structure paragraphs in which a topic sentence (GS) is explained or supported by three or four specific ideas (SP's). But, as you have already discovered, it is not enough to write down your three or four specific ideas in sentence form following the topic sentence. If you do, the paragraph that results is likely to sound more like a grocery list than a smoothly flowing paragraph.

For example, consider the following paragraph diagram that one student writer produced:

> GS: A hobby can often pay big dividends for those who invest their time in it.
> SP: It can make boredom a thing of the past.
> SP: It adds to one's feeling of self-esteem.
> SP: It can bring one into contact with new and interesting people.
> SP: It can sometimes be financially profitable.

If the writer had merely written down the specific ideas one after another following the topic sentence, the resulting paragraph would have sounded awkward and incomplete:

> A hobby can often pay big dividends for those who invest their time in it. For one thing, it can make boredom a thing of the past. It also adds to one's feelings of self-esteem. Third, a hobby can bring one into contact with new and interesting people. Perhaps the greatest payoff, though, is that sometimes a hobby can be financially profitable.

What the writer has produced is a list in paragraph form, not a complete paragraph. A list is only useful as a reminder to the person who wrote it. Hence, a grocery list taken to the store by the person who listed the items is likely to serve its purpose:

    Groceries:
      coffee
      lima beans
      bread
      ice cream

If, however, the grocery list is being prepared by one shopper for another
(as when a mother sends her teenaged son to the market), a list of bare
items will not be effective. Additional explanation is essential.

    Groceries:
      coffee
        be sure to get the large red can (If it's over $3.00, get the small size)
      lima beans
        not the big fat ones—the small ones (In a box, please, not a bag)
      bread
        something for sandwiches—two loaves, anything but pumpernickel
      ice cream
        chocolate or strawberry, not vanilla (Dairy creme is usually the
        cheapest)

To communicate effectively, the items on the grocery list must be
explained with additional details. Similarly, the specific ideas (SP's) in
a paragraph must be amplified with additional details. These are what
are lacking in the student's paragraph on the benefits of hobbies on the
previous page. The paragraph can be improved immensely by the
addition of at least one sentence after each SP, explaining, qualifying or
in some way extending the meaning of the supporting statement.

These additional sentences will be referred to in this text as
extenders. They provide the "meat" that turns the bare bones of
paragraph diagram from a list into a paragraph. Here is how the
paragraph on hobbies looks with the addition of an *extender* after each
SP:

> A hobby can often pay big dividends for those who invest their time
> in it. For one thing, it can make boredom a thing of the past. The hobby
> fills empty hours with interesting, constructive activity. It also adds to
> feelings of self-esteem. Knowing that one is an expert at something
> increases confidence. Third, a hobby can bring one into contact with new
> and interesting people. Others who share the same hobby are an excellent
> source of friendship. Perhaps the greatest payoff, though, is that sometimes
> a hobby can be financially profitable. Items made or skills developed are
> often in great demand, and selling these can be a source of extra income.

Compare the paragraph above with the earlier version that did not
include extenders. Can you detect how much more smoothly the paragraph reads and how much more complete the ideas are?

Here is a paragraph diagram for the paragraph on hobbies, with
the extenders (EX) included:

GS: A hobby can often pay big dividends for those who invest their time in it.
SP: It can make boredom a thing of the past.
    EX: fills empty hours with constructive activity
SP: It also adds to feelings of self-esteem.
    EX: Knowing that one's an expert gives confidence.
SP: Hobby can bring one into contact with new people.
    EX: Others who share the hobby are good friends.
SP: Hobby can be financially profitable.
    EX: Items made or skills developed can be sold.

The formula for paragraphs in this book will require that each supporting statement (each SP) be followed by at least one sentence that gives information that is even more specific than the SP and helps explain it. A paragraph following this format will be comprised of at least three levels of specificity: The topic sentence (GS) will be the most general statement in the paragraph. The supporting statements (SP's) will be less general (more specific) than the topic sentence. These, in turn, will each be followed by one or more extenders (EX's) that are even less general (more specific) than the supporting statements (SP's). If you follow this formula for your developed paragraphs, it is unlikely that you will ever be criticized for failure to develop your subject adequately.

• EXERCISE A

In each of the paragraphs below, identify the topic sentence (general statement), the supporting specifics, and the extender sentences following each of the supporting specifics. Underline the topic sentence, number the specifics, and mark the extenders with "Ex." Then fill in the paragraph diagram that follows each paragraph, using brief phrases if space does not permit writing complete sentences.

1.   It is relatively easy to improve the coherence of one's writing. A few simple techniques which anyone can adopt will make an immediate difference. The use of logical connectors, for example, or transitional devices, as they are sometimes called, is an aid to clear, logical writing. Readers need all the help they can get, and a well-placed "however," "for example," or "therefore" can add immeasureably to ease of reading. The use of pronouns is another simple means of improving coherence. Every pronoun correctly used refers to an antecedent in the same or preceding sentence and serves, in effect, to weave the writing together, as in a mesh. A third way even a novice writer can make writing flow logically and fluently is to develop the habit of consistency. The writer who begins a

paragraph writing about "people" should stick with "people," and not switch to "a person" or "you" or "we"; and a narrative begun in the past tense should not switch to the present tense or to the future conditional for no apparent reason. Even more important, however, than all of these means of achieving coherence in writing is the habit of filling in all the gaps in thinking. The writer who depends on the reader's willingness to infer what is not said is asking a great deal, and even a skillful and interested reader is likely to feel that the author has not provided a complete and lucid piece of writing.

GS _____

_____

SP _____

EX _____

SP _____

EX _____

SP _____

EX _____

SP _____

EX _____

2.   The club consisted of four distinct groups of personalities. Most vocal were those members who were totally devoted to the president and supported her in everything she suggested. The president had only to make her wishes known and these obedient followers immediately wheeled into line behind her, marshalling arguments and hustling votes. One got the impression that they would vote for their own execution if the president called for it. These members were opposed, of course, by an equally vigorous group which automatically disapproved of any plan that emanated from the president's camp. They would have vetoed their own elevation to the peerage if their nomination had come from the president or one of her supporters. A third group of members, less serious in intent, enjoyed themselves by stirring up trouble, asking questions with embarrassing answers and bringing up subjects the more earnest members would rather have left buried. They had no real interest in how issues were settled or which faction controlled the group; they simply enjoyed thrusting themselves forward in ways that discomfited the leaders. Their antics saved the day for the fourth group, comprised of inert individuals

antics saved the day for the fourth group, comprised of inert individuals who were not even interested enough to cause trouble, but who sometimes roused themselves enough to cast the deciding vote for the group whose performance pleased them most. They were a group to be reckoned with, a group whose power to determine the future of the club far exceeded any contribution they made to it.

GS _____

_____

SP _____

EX _____

SP _____

EX _____

SP _____

EX _____

SP _____

EX _____

Check your answers on p. 172 before continuing.

• EXERCISE B

In the following paragraphs only the topic sentence (GS) and the main ideas supporting the topic sentence (SP's) have been included. Fill in the blanks with *extenders* of some kind in order to turn these bare "grocery lists" into completely developed paragraphs.

1.   While television shows are reasonably good, the commercials that accompany them are a disgrace. One of the many bad features of commercials is their loudness. _____

_____

_____

_____ . Commercials take up too much time and are repeated too often. _____

_____

_____

_____ . Often

commercials interrupt a show at a particularly inappropriate time. _____

_____

_____

_____ . Too many commercials insult the viewer's
intelligence by presenting unrealistic situations and senseless dialogue.

_____

_____

_____

2.   Every season of the year brings its gift of beauty to the lover of
nature. Spring offers welcome delights that make it the favorite season of

many.   _____

_____

_____

Summer offers a very different kind of beauty, more lively, bright and

vigorous.   _____

_____

_____

_____ . Autumn's beauty has a dual
nature, expressing the ripeness of harvest along with the sense of ending,

of closing down for winter, that follows. _____

_____

_____

_____ . Even winter,
for all its absense of vividness and growth, has colors of its own that give

particular pleasure to the sensitive beholder. _____

_____

_____

_____

Check the Answer Key on p. 173 before continuing.

• EXERCISE C

Check the paragraphs you wrote for Steps 10 and 12 to see whether you have provided adequate *extenders* following each specific detail. Does your paragraph sound like a grocery list or is it a unified whole? Have your extenders provided details that are even more specific than the SP's they follow? Sometimes it is difficult to detect these things in your own work. Ask a friend to read your paragraph for this purpose and to indicate where you need additional explanatory material to develop your specific ideas in more detail. Then rework these spots and copy the paragraphs over in final form.

STEP 14 — Writing a Complete Paragraph

• EXERCISE

Carefully plan and write a paragraph, following the steps below and checking them off as you do them.

_____1. Choose one of the following subjects, or a similar one assigned or approved by your instructor.
  a) Courtesy—Is It Really Necessary?
  b) Definition of a Good Sport
  c) Benefits of Regular Exercise
  d) Successful Dieting
  e) Male Chauvinism—A Fact of Life in America?
  f) Creating the Perfect Banana Split

_____2. Using the following chart, plan your paragraph. Write a topic sentence (GS) about the subject in the blank provided. Make sure it is a complete sentence and shows your opinion on some aspect of the topic. Then list three or four specifics which support, explain or illustrate your topic sentence.

GS _____

_____

SP _____

SP _____

SP _____

SP _____

_____3. Check your list of specifics to make sure they are all directly related to your general statement. Do they all help to prove or explain it? If any of your specifics do not belong, cross them out. Add any others you think of.

_____4. Write your paragraph in the space provided below, being sure to explain each specific statement with one or two extender sentences containing whatever material is needed to develop your ideas.

_____

_____

_____

_____

_____

_____

_____

_____

_____

_____

_____

_____

_____

_____

_____

_____

_____

_____

_____

_____

_____

_____

_____5. Check your paragraph for any errors in grammar, punctuation, and spelling. Then underline the topic sentence and number the specifics and write "Ex" before each extender. Of course, you will not always do this last step in writing a paragraph to turn in to your teacher. But, when practicing, it helps you to visualize the structure of your paragraph.

Check the Answer Key on p. 174 before continuing.

III

Giving Other Shapes to the Paragraph

<table>
<tr><td>STEP
15</td><td>**Positioning the General Statement**</td></tr>
</table>

In all exercises thus far, you have placed the general statement (the topic sentence) at the beginning of your paragraph and have followed it with your supporting particulars. This order is called *deductive* and is effective for most paragraphs. Sometimes, however, it is useful to reverse this procedure and open a paragraph with particulars which lead to a summarizing generalization at the end of the paragraph. This particular-to-general order is called *inductive* and is especially helpful if the writer wishes to lead a wary reader through a series of persuasive details to what might be a controversial conclusion. Here is an example of a paragraph with the topic sentence at the end.

Cats have a disarming way of sidling up to a person whose attention they want, looking sidewise and pretending a lack of interest. They seldom approach frontally, bounding cheerfully, as would a dog, asking openly to be petted. Rather, cats will sit down a short distance away and stare intently in another direction, as if the last thing they could possibly want is to be petted or picked up. If given the slightest bit of encouragement, however, they approach casually, strolling as if with no particular aim, and end up near the target person, willing to rub softly against extended legs or even to leap into a lap if an invitation is extended. Once sure of scratching hand and rub and butt and curl and twist to take full advantage of affection afforded. They purr like little motors to express their own affection and appreciation. <u>Cats, in short, are not less man's friend than dogs; they are simply more subtle in their manner.</u> (Topic sentence is underlined.)

Sometimes it is useful to place the generalization or topic sentence at the beginning of the paragraph in order to let the reader know immediately what the paragraph is about, and then to restate the generalization at the end as a summary and conclusion. This type can be thought of as a *sandwich paragraph*, since the specifics are "sandwiched" in between two statements of a general idea. (The general statement at the end is often called a *clincher* sentence because it ties together the details in the paragraph.) Here is an example of a sandwich paragraph. It begins with a general statement (topic sentence), then presents supporting details, and concludes with a restatement of the general idea (clincher).

> <u>Parents should guide their children in growing up.</u> While children are still quite young, they should be given a few simple responsibilities, such as keeping themselves clean without always having to be told to do so. Later, parents should help their children learn to manage some of their other affairs, such as budgeting their allowance and deciding on a sensible bedtime. By the time children reach adolescence, parents should have prepared them for the more important decisions they will have to make—whether they want to go to college, whether to experiment with drugs, and how to handle sexual freedom. <u>Learning to accept responsibility, to manage one's own affairs, and to make one's own moral and professional decisions are important steps in growing up, and parents have an obligation to prepare their children to take them.</u> (Topic sentence and clincher underlined.)

• EXERCISE A

In each paragraph below, underline the topic sentence (general statement). It may be at the beginning, or at the end, or in some cases at the beginning with a clincher at the end (if so, underline both).

1. The owner of a pet alligator should protect it by placing it in a pen of some sort. The most dangerous enemies of such a pet are human beings. Young neighborhood children will attempt to do away with the murky green reptile by squeezing and squishing it, by feeding it inedible items, by stoning it, or simply by scaring it to death. Other animals are also adversaries of a pet alligator. Both cats and dogs will be curious about this strange looking creature. When investigating it to satisfy their curiosity, they may challenge the alligator. Still another major threat to its existence in civilization is traffic. Nowadays, with the increase in cars,

trucks, and bicycles, the chances of survival for a pet alligator on the loose are not good. All of these dangers can be eliminated if the owner keeps the pet in a fenced-off pond or in a pen.

2.   A snowfall in late spring brings a special excitement as two seasons manifest themselves at once. The dark boughs of trees and bushes, just beginning to bud, turn into popcorn boughs as the wet, fluffy snow clings to every joint and twig. Beneath the trees, where snow is sparse, a circle of vivid green spreads outward and fades gradually into the white ground cover. The unseasonable white seems more white than winter snow, and the green more brilliant than grass can be. In our usual experience, snow lies against the black of wet winter boughs, and the shock of white against the colors of spring is unforgettable once seen. White sprinkled on the yellow of forsythia and burdening the bright red sprays of blooming quince completes a bouquet more beautiful for its unexpectedness. The balm in the air makes clear that spring will win this encounter. Already the snow is melting into the earth, turning the ground darker and the grass more green. Spring snow is short lived.

3.   A home decorating precept worth considering is that every room should contain something alive. It is altogether too easy for a room to become an inert collection of fabrics, woods and plastics, and anything which can instill a sense of animation and growth makes an important addition. Indoor plants are an easy beginning. The homemaker need not be a skilled gardener to add a cactus garden to a table top or hang a basket of shade-loving ivy in a corner. Large tropical plants in floor tubs placed against a wall or in a corner form a dramatic background for furniture and lend a sense of jungle liveliness. In some rooms an aquarium can illuminate an otherwise dull area, providing light and movement which attract and please the eye. The underwater plants and darting fish, brilliant under the aquarium light, truly bring life to a room. Another possibility is a bird in a hanging cage. Perhaps such an idea is not suitable for a formal drawing room, but a kitchen or family room is made livelier by installing a cheerful little chirper to keep the family company.

4.   If you are to learn to study efficiently, you must become a good notetaker. When it is time to take notes, do not grab any piece of paper that happens to be handy and begin to scribble. Instead, keep a special section of your notebook for all your notes on each subject. Label each set of notes with the class, the date, and the name of the lecture so that you will be able to put it back in its logical order should you have to remove it from the notebook for some reason. For maximum efficiency, make a real effort to discriminate between the important and the trivial in what you hear. Do not just write all you can, as fast as you can. Instead, listen for main points and supporting details. Putting your notes in outline

form is also helpful. Avoid the "stream of consciousness" style that so many students use—long paragraphs of unrelated ideas, including cryptographic notations of the various comments made by the instructor. You will find it helpful to look over your notes as soon as possible after taking them in order to revise or rewrite them intelligently. This step prevents the horrible realization the night before a test that, "My notes just don't make sense!"

5.   Everywhere they turn today Americans are confronted with the message that they can stay youthful forever. Television, the all-persuasive conveyor of values, bombards viewers with reassurance that youthful beauty can last forever. The right face cream, the right formula to put glowing color in the hair, the ultimate girdle for maintaining the body beautiful—all these present tested ways to hold age at bay. If cosmetics fail, there is always medicine. There is a pill for every purpose; if one is tired or distraught or bored, a pill can come to the rescue. Magazines assure their readers that an active sex life need not end with the middle years but can flourish even to the grave. One can be romantic even with dentures and full of gaiety and excitement even beyond the youthful norm if one drinks the right soft drink, uses the best hearing aid and attends a sufficient number of lectures on inner awareness. Americans are beguiled into thinking they will become, at worst, as old looking and old feeling as the thirty-five year old models who do the Geritol and Anacin commercials. Old age, obviously, is for other people.

6.   Joan's greatest disappointment was the time she went to a dude ranch in Utah for her vacation. When she first arrived, it was night and she could not see well enough to get a good overall impression. However, she could clearly see the small cabin with only one window and a broken door which let in cold air every night. She had to sleep under all the blankets she could find in the cabin and pile her coat on top. Even so, she was miserable all night. In the morning, she rose early and walked down to the stables, eager to see the horses and the facilities for riding. To her dismay, she saw nothing that resembled the pictures she had seen in the advertising pamphlet the dude ranch had sent her. Those pictures showed beautiful new stables and a riding ring in perfect condition, whereas the reality was far less attractive, consisting of unpainted buildings, broken down fences, and weed choked bridle trails. The advertising pictures, she realized, must have been taken many years before. Her dismay increased when she discovered that the ranch had far fewer horses than it had guests, and she would not be able to ride nearly as often as she had planned. Fortunately, the scenery was beautiful, and she was able to take long hikes in the upland meadows near the ranch house. She was grateful for such pleasures; however, that vacation remained in her memory as a dismal and disappointing experience.

7.   The Gateway Arch, a national monument to the westward expansion movement, is located on the Mississippi River in downtown St. Louis. The curve of the arch is 630 feet high and can be seen from as far as twenty miles away. The train that takes visitors to the top for sightseeing is itself a remarkable engineering feat. The seats remain upright like those on a ferris wheel as the cars are pulled up one leg of the horseshoe curve of the arch to an observation room high above the city. The view at the top is breathtaking, with every building, smokestack and major street in St. Louis and across the river in East St. Louis clearly visible on a sunny day. Hundreds of thousands of tourists from every country in the world have made the trip to the top of the arch and have then visited the spacious area underground beneath the arch. Two movie theaters, an impressive fountain in the center of a large lobby, a museum, and numerous other facilities and displays are located underground at the base of the arch. This truly spectacular tourist attraction is well worth a special trip to St. Louis.

8.   The starting time of a sports event is often delayed or changed because of television. Such an instance occurred last fall in a college football game between Syracuse and Penn State. The game was being televised, and ABC network control personnel thought it would be best if the game were started forty-five minutes late so that more viewers would be attracted. Unfortunately, the stadium did not have any lights, and by the end of the game the two teams were groping around in the dark. An equally disturbing event involved Southern Methodist University and Texas A and M. For the last twenty-two years these teams have traditionally clashed on Thanksgiving Day. This year, however, they met on September 16th, just so the game could be televised.

9.   Typing is much less fatiguing than handwriting, especially when one uses an electric typewriter. One can typewrite for hours without fatigue, while steady writing for a time will often produce writer's cramp. Also, no matter how tired one becomes, the character of typed letters never changes. Script, on the other hand, tends to get sloppy after long periods of writing. Furthermore, typing is always legible with a minimum of effort. At times personal script is so poor that it is difficult, if not impossible, to read. Legibility can contribute to an improved grade, since a teacher is more likely to give a low grade to a sloppily written paper than to a neat, typewritten one. The biggest advantage, however, is speed. A good typist can type from forty to seventy words per minute, while only about twenty to thirty words per minute can be written legibly by hand. Every student, therefore, should learn to type because of the many advantages which typing has over script.

Check your answers on p. 175 before continuing.

• EXERCISE B

Carefully plan and write a paragraph, placing the topic sentence at the *end*. Follow these steps, checking them off as you go:

_____ 1. Choose one of the following subjects or a similar one assigned or approved by your instructor:
   a) Advantages of Inter-generational Friendships
   b) People Who Irritate Me
   c) What I Want in a Friend
   d) What It Takes to Be a Good Athlete
   e) How to Lose a Job

_____ 2. Using the chart below, plan your paragraph. Write a topic sentence (GS) about the subject in the blank provided. Make sure it is a complete sentence and shows your opinion on some aspect of the subject. Then list three or four specifics which support, explain or illustrate your topic sentence.

GS _____

_____

SP _____

SP _____

SP _____

SP _____

_____ 3. Check to make sure that all of your specifics are directly related to your general statement. Do they all help to prove or explain it? If any of them do not belong, cross them out. Add any others you can think of.

_____ 4. Write your paragraph in the space provided, placing the general statement at the end. (You will, therefore, begin the paragraph with the first specific, not the topic sentence.) Be sure to follow each specific statement with one or two extender sentences containing whatever material is needed to explain and develop your ideas. Use any "lead-in" expression, such as *therefore*, *hence*, or *then* needed to connect the specifics and the general statement.

_____

_____

_____

_____

_____

_____

_____

_____

_____

_____

_____

_____

_____

_____

_____

_____

_____

_____

_____

_____

_____

_____

_____

___5. Check your paragraph for any errors in grammar, punctuation, and spelling. Then underline the topic sentence, number the specifics, and write "Ex" before each extender sentence.

Check the Answer Key on p. 175 before continuing.

• EXERCISE C

Plan and write a *sandwich* paragraph, placing the topic sentence at the *beginning* and rephrasing the general statement in a clincher sentence at the *end*. Follow these steps, checking them off as you go.

___1. Choose one of the following topics or a similar one assigned or approved by your instructor:
a) How to Enjoy a Weekend

   b) The Role of Prison in Society: Retribution or Reform?
   c) The Good (or Bad) Effects of Commercial TV on Children
   d) The Art of Friendship
   e) On Being (or Not Being) a Vegetarian

_____2. Using the chart below, plan your paragraph. Write a general state-
       ment about your subject in the space provided. Make sure it is a
       complete sentence and shows your attitude toward some aspect of
       the topic. Then list three or four specifics which support, explain or
       illustrate your topic sentence.

   GS _____

   _____

       SP _____
       SP _____
       SP _____
       SP _____.

_____3. Check your list of specifics to make sure they are all directly related
       to your general statement. Eliminate any that are not. Add any
       others that occur to you.

_____4. Write the paragraph in the space provided below, placing the topic
       sentence at the beginning. Be sure to explain each specific state-
       ment with one or two extender sentences.

   _____

   _____

   _____

   _____

   _____

   _____

   _____

   _____

   _____

   _____

_____

_____

_____

_____

_____

_____

_____

_____

_____

_____

_____

_____

_____5. Conclude your paragraph with a *clincher* statement—a restatement of the general idea in different words from the topic sentence and written in such a way as to make your paragraph sound "finished."

_____6. Check your paragraph for any errors in grammar, punctuation, and spelling. Then underline the topic sentence and the clincher sentence, number the specifics, and write "Ex" before each extender sentence.

Check the Answer Key on p. 175 before continuing.

STEP 16 — Using Four Types of Specifics

It cannot be emphasized too strongly that a writer's primary obligation is to develop all general ideas with specific details. The use of specifics to support a topic sentence is called *paragraph development,* and one of the requirements of a good paragraph is, of course, that it be developed in sufficient detail to make the topic idea entirely clear to the audience the writer is addressing.

The best way to be sure a paragraph will be well developed is to plan ahead of time the specifics (the supporting statements) that are to be used, and a good way to be sure of having effective specifics come to mind when one needs them is to become familiar with the various *kinds* of specifics that are available to writers. Writers who are fully conscious of a wide variety of means of development are in a good position to choose the most effective means to develop the particular topic sentence they have at hand.

Expository writing very often consists of paragraphs developed by the following means:

1) examples, illustrations
2) facts, statistics, data
3) an incident
4) reasons

This step will acquaint you with these four common means of developing paragraphs.

It is important to know that the nature of the topic sentence usually determines the means of developing that will prove most useful. Note how, in each of the following examples, the topic sentence clearly lends itself to the *kind* of specifics used.

Examples, Illustrations. An example is one instance or case used to illustrate an entire group. Each of the specifics given below is an example of the "different forms" of soap mentioned in the general statement.

> GS It is possible to buy soap in many different forms.
> SP Cake soap is milled and pressed into a hard, long-lasting cake.
> SP Bar soap is cut from a huge slab of soap by long knives.
> SP Flake soap is scraped from a slab in small, flat pieces.
> SP Powdered soap is formed by condensing crystals on the cold surface of a cooling tower.

Facts, Statistics, Data. Each of the specifics given below is a fact or statistic which helps to prove the general statement. (A fact is a statement of something that exists or occurs which can be verified through observation. Statistics and data are the expression of facts in numbers.)

> GS Although nearly every war has been fought with the idea that it would be the last, the history of civilization has proved otherwise.
> SP From 1500 B.C. to 1860 A.D., there were at least 8000 wars.
> SP Since 650 B.C., there have been 1656 arms races, all but sixteen ending in actual hostilities.

SP In the 150 years after 1776, Great Britain alone was involved in 54 wars, lasting a total of 102 years.

SP During that time, France was engaged in 53 wars, lasting for 99 years.

SP The United States was almost continually in one kind of battle or another: the Revolution, the War of 1812, the Civil War, wars against Indians, the Mexican War, the Spanish-American War, World Wars I and II, and military actions in Mexico, Haiti, Nicaragua, the Dominican Republic, Cuba, and Southeast Asia.

An Incident. Each of the specifics below tells part of a story which explains or justifies the general statement.

GS I have always been wary of airplane travel, and with good reason.

SP I remember my first flight on a commercial airline.

SP It was on a DC-3 from Topeka, Kansas, to Stillwater, Oklahoma.

SP The stewardess was as nervous as I.

SP She assured me, however, that the plane could land in a cornfield if necessary—and we almost did!

SP Despite the rough flying, I manfully ate my dinner—much to my regret.

SP Our landing gear stuck, and we had to circle Stillwater airport using up fuel, before an emergency landing.

Explanation by Reasons. When the general statement leads the reader to ask "why?," it needs to be explained with reasons, such as those in the example below:

GS One should learn the basic facts of nutrition before becoming a vegetarian.

SP to determine what kind or degree of vegetarianism to embrace

SP to learn the main food groups essential to good health

SP to learn how to maintain protein level of diet

SP to learn comparative calorie counts of foods substituted for those relinquished.

• EXERCISE A

Some topic sentences lend themselves to development by more than one kind of specific, and when this is the case a combination of specifics is often useful. In the examples below, label each of the specifics as an example, fact, incident, or reason. In deciding, notice the way in which each specific relates to the topic sentence. (Some of the specifics may fall into more than one category.)

1. Topic Sentence: The hospital's parking facilities badly need immediate improvement.

a) —————————SP Only 50 percent of the employees can park at one time.

b) —————————SP Lack of lighting makes the nurses feel nervous when they come and go for late shifts.

c) —————————SP One day last week, three visiting doctors arrived to find the lot completely full. They drove around and around the lot for at least fifteen minutes, hoping to find an empty space. Finally in exasperation, one of them leapt from the car and dashed into the hospital, where he collared the first orderly he spied and compelled him to go out and get in the car and find a parking space, so the doctors could reach their meeting on time.

d) —————————SP A 300-bed hospital needs more than the 15,000 square feet of parking provided in 1939, prior to two expansion programs.

e) —————————SP Unless doctors on the day shift arrive before 7:00 A.M., they are likely to find no parking places left.

f) —————————SP The cost of paving is increasing 10 percent annually.

2. Topic Sentence: Cigarette smoking is harmful.

a) —————————SP The report on smoking of the Surgeon-General of the United States reveals that smoking increases the likelihood of lung cancer, emphysema, and high blood pressure.

b) —————————SP I had no idea smoking was harming me in any way until I decided to take up running as a hobby. The first time I tried to run a half mile without stopping, I found myself puffing and panting like a much older, heavier person. On the suggestion of a friend, I quit smoking for a few days and, to my amazement, found an almost immediate improvement in my wind. Needless to say, I never resumed smoking.

c) —————————SP My expenses for cigarettes total amost $400 a year.

d) —————————SP Smoking deprives one of much enjoyment in life. A habitual smoker cannot taste a good steak nor smell a flower.

e) —————————SP Present research indicates a causal relationship between smoking and signs of early aging.

3. Topic Sentence: His early political success gave a badly needed boost to his self-esteem.

a) ——————SP He had never thought he could achieve success in his father's field.

b) ——————SP Having twenty-three thousand people vote for him made him feel very good.

c) —————— SP He discovered during his campaign that he was a natural orator and crowd pleaser.

d) ——————SP He was fearful, at first, before large rallies. He feared, on one occasion, that he would be heckled by rowdies. He need not have worried. The crowd expelled his hecklers and cheered him to the rafters. He realized he had found his true calling.

e) ——————SP The papers called him the "boy wonder" of the local party.

Check your answers on p. 175 before continuing.

• EXERCISE B

Underline the topic sentence (and clincher, if there is one) in each paragraph below. Then decide how each paragraph has been developed (what kind of specifics it contains). Only one type has been used in each paragraph. Write your answer in the space provided.

1. The English language is full of words borrowed from Latin. The prefix *com-* (meaning "with" or "together") is found in such words as *command, compass, commission, compact,* and *compare.* The knowledge of the Latin word *cedere,* meaning "to yield" or "to go," helps to reveal the meanings of the English words *cessation, cession, accede, access, ancestor, concede, exceed, incessant, precede, procedure, process, recede,* and *succeed,* as well as many others. Knowing the prefix *uni-* (meaning "one") can enhance one's understanding of newspaper articles about *unilateral* disarmament, for example. The root *voc-* (meaning "call") gives a key to one's study of *vocabulary.* In short, a study of Latin words can help one expand one's knowledge immensely and become a more literate person.
Type of Specifics ————————————————————

2. The community as a whole seemed to be satisfied with the administrators' higher salary levels. Most parents in the district recognized the

seriousness of the responsibilities the administrators had to cope with daily. They evidently felt that the safety and educational welfare of their children were extremely important matters, and they were willing to pay top salaries to those whose task it was to maintain them. Parents whose children had come through the district's schools from kindergarten to high school had become personally familiar with at least three of the thirteen buildings that belonged to the district. Many of them had joined in campaigning for bond issues and tax increases to build schools for the expanding community, and they wanted competent and knowledge-able people taking care of those schools. They knew, also, that the faculties of the district were considered to be superior to those of nearby districts, and they wanted to keep the administrators who had established those faculties and who had made the district a happy place for a competent teacher to work. As business people themselves, the members of the school board had no illusions as to what would happen if they allowed administrators' salaries to lag behind those of other districts. They wanted top people, and they were willing to pay for them.

Type of Specifics _____

3.   It has been proven fairly conclusively that the radioactive fallout from nuclear accidents or weapons testing shortens the life span of individual organisms. Analysis of death rates in the United States by the Compertz function shows that, for men, the normal life expectancy under normal conditions is cut in half after every increase in age of eight years. Exposure to radiation increases the death rate by shifting the curve of this function to the left. This shift means that the life span will be cut in proportion to the amount of the shift. In particular, a dose of 300 roentgens of radiation shortens the life span by four to nine days per roentgen. Even though the effects are reduced when the dose is spread out over a long period of time, as in the case of fallout, the inescapable conclusion is that radiation affects a population so that its members die off from all causes at earlier ages than they would in a radiation-free environment.

Type of Specifics _____

4.   The life of the average citizen in an underdeveloped country is far from pleasant. Only 1 out of 3 can read or write. Hundreds of millions live on a dollar a week. The average income is less that $2.50 a week— or $140 a year. (In the United States it is $2800.) Citizens of underdeveloped countries live an average of thirty-six years; in the United States and Europe the life expectancy is almost twice that—sixty-seven years. In 1950, malaria killed a million babies in India alone. Three out of 5 people in Latin America were discovered never to have had a glass of pure water, and 1000 children a day were dying as a result. Fifty-five out of every 100 children in Guatemala died before the age of four. Thirty

million Brazilians did not own a pair of shoes. Hundreds of millions of people in the poorer countries of the world suffered from trachoma, bilharzia, dysentery, anemia, tuberculosis, malaria, leprosy, yaws, and other diseases. Few had a decent roof over their heads. Most lived in mud or bamboo huts.
Type of Specifics _____

5.   One often sees good evidence that men are as poor at driving as women are assumed to be. Once, as I was driving up to an intersection, the car in front of me—driven by a man—stopped short. I slammed on my brakes and narrowly avoided a collision. Since the light was green, I honked my horn in an attempt to get him to move. As he started to roll slowly forward, the light changed to yellow. He immediately put on his brakes and stopped in the middle of the intersection. I stopped a short distance behind him to enable him to back up. The next thing I knew, the man's car was moving backwards toward mine at about 20 miles per hour. Before I even had time to honk my horn again, he slammed into my car, giving me a painful whiplash injury—a painful reminder that women hold no monopoly on poor driving.
Type of Specifics _____

6.   An improvement in one's vocabulary can be helpful in a number of ways. Knowing synonyms for words, for instance, will decrease the amount of repetition in one's writing and make it more enjoyable to read. If editors enjoy reading one's articles and find them lively and original, they will surely pay a higher price for them. Also, an increased vocabulary makes one's own reading more enjoyable. It is much easier to follow the ideas in a book or in the newspapers when one does not have to run to run continually to the dictionary to look up unknown words. Eliminating such constant interruptions surely makes a person more eager to read and less likely to give up entirely when an occasional unknown work is encountered. A broad familiarity with the language will enable one to read more swiftly and more intelligently, become more knowledgeable, and relate more usefully to the world. Strange as it may seem, vocabulary study can make one a better person.
Type of Specifics _____

7.   It is a common human tendency to avoid making decisions even in trivial matters before checking out one's intentions with someone else. No matter that the other person is no wiser or better informed; at least there is the comfort of a shared viewpoint. I learned recently, at some cost, that this behavior is really not very rational or helpful. I had been invited to a reception for a renowed literary figure who would be visiting St. Louis, and my delight at receiving such an unexpected honor was tempered only by my trepidation over what I should wear. I discussed

my uncertainty with a close friend, who, like me, had never been to such an affair. She had, however, seen many such occasions in movies and was quite positive that I should plan to dress very formally. A floor-length gown was *de rigueur*. Since her opinion was compatible with my own love of dressing up, I found it easy to accept her advice and embarked on a shopping spree of serious dimensions. The day before the reception, when I had committed several upcoming paychecks to my formal costume, I ran into the acquaintance who had arranged the invitation for me. I thanked her, and we chatted briefly. As she moved away, she called back, "Be sure to dress comfortably. Mr. X hasn't been out of jeans since he was born." Bless her heart, and bless the luck that made her cross my path that day! She was right; the reception was about as formal as a barbecue, and as I sat on the floor cracking peanut shells I vowed never again to ask for advice from someone who is just as ignorant as I am.

Type of Specifics ―――――――――――――――――――――

8.　　One cause of prejudice in our society is the lack of contact between different ethnic, cultural, and economic groups. People who earn about the same amount of money usually live in the same neighborhoods and stick together socially. People with similar cultural and educational backgrounds—especially immigrants and racial minorities—are very often isolated from the rest of society because they are not accepted by other groups as equals and because they feel happier and safer with those who share the same background and problems. When groups become isolated from each other in this way, fear and distruct build up, for people who have no social contact with those who are different from themselves can only guess and generalize about the reasons why they act as they do; and more often than not they draw wrong conclusions from ignorance. Nothing is more likely to produce prejudice than trying to judge ideas and behavior about which one knows nothing.

Type of Specifics ―――――――――――――――――――――

9.　　Some of the simplest of life's lessons seem to be learnable only through experience—at least in my case. I blush when I recall how glibly I criticized "get well" cards as commercial and impersonal, and the gift of flowers to the ill as impractical if not downright frivolous. I hope no one was listening, for I now know how mistaken I was. Two years ago I underwent surgery and was kept in the hospital for ten days. The first day after my operation, when I was wired up to numerous gadgets and could not have moved even if I had been strong enough, a gray haired lady in a pink uniform came into my room with a friendly smile and a stack of mail—yes, "get well" cards. I received them as if they had been life-saving medicine and at once started to feel better. Perhaps I would decide to survive after all. Each day, I watched for that pink lady, and as the pile of cards grew, I read them over and over and showed them to my visitors. And the flowers? Impractical they may have been, but only as a tonic is impractical and only as loving words are impractical in time of need. I saved each blossom until it was wilted beyond reclaiming, and even then, pressed a few to keep. They remind me of a lesson I needed to learn: expressions of love are welcome in any form.

Type of Specifics _____

10.   Although most people are aware of the high crime rate in this country and the fact that thousands of people are sentenced to prison each year, few have any knowledge of the conditions of prison life. There are about two hundred and fifty thousand persons in prisons in the United States. In general, their sentences are longer than any in the Western World. Their lives are harsh and isolated. Many spend long hours doing strenuous manual labor on state farms, yet are given no skills which will enable them to adjust to the outside world. The emotional problems of some make it necessary to keep them in solitary confinement—usually in cells no larger than 5 feet by 9. As the facilities for rehabilitating prisoners are extremely limited, many return to prison life again and again. All of these factors seem to point to a self-perpetuating prison system—a sad fact which all too few Americans are aware of or concerned about.

Type of Specifics _____

Check your answers on p. 175 before continuing.

• EXERCISE C

Plan and write a paragraph developed by *facts and statistics.* Follow these steps, checking them off as you go.

_____ 1. Choose one of the following subjects or a similar one assigned or approved by your instructor:
    a) Alcoholism—Its Cost in Human Life
    b) Causes of Highway Accidents
    c) Oxygen—Essential for the Human Body
    d) The Effects of Tranquilizers (or some other drug)
    e) Our Basketball Team's Fine (or Bad) Season
    f) America's Greed (or Need) for Oil
    g) Influenza—More Serious Than Most People Realize
    h) Juvenile Crime

_____ 2. Using the following chart, plan your paragraph. Write a general statement about your subject in the space provided. List the specific *facts and statistics* which explain or prove your topic sentence. (You may have to get your information from a reference book or other outside source.)

GS _____

_____

SP _____

SP _____

SP _____

SP _____

_____3. Check to make sure that all your specific details (*facts and statistics*) support your general statement directly. Eliminate any that do not. Add any that occur to you later.

_____4. In the space provided below, write your paragraph. Be sure to add an extender sentence or two after each specific statement to amplify or explain it.

_____

_____

_____

_____

_____

_____

_____

_____

_____

_____

_____

_____

_____

_____

_____

_____

_____

_____

_____

_____

_____

_____

___ 5. Check your paragraph for any errors in grammar, punctuation, and spelling. Then underline the topic sentence (and clincher if you have used one) and number the specifics. Label with "Ex" the extender sentences.

Check the Answer Key on p. 175 before continuing.

• EXERCISE D

Plan and write a paragraph developed by *examples*. Follow these steps, checking them off as you go.

___ 1. Choose one of the following topics or a similar one assigned or approved by your instructor.
   a) What I Like Most About My Parents
   b) TV Commercials I Admire (or Dislike)
   c) How I've Changed in the Last Year
   d) Careers of the Future

___ 2. Using the following chart, plan your paragraph. Write a general statement about your subject in the space provided. List *examples* which illustrate it.

GS _____

_____

SP _____

SP _____

SP _____

SP _____

___3. Check to make sure that all your specific details are directly related to your general statement. Eliminate any that are not. Add any new ones that occur to you.

___4. In the space provided below, write your paragraph. After each sentence introducing an example, add one or more *extenders* to explain or furnish additional details about the example.

_____

_____

_____

_____

_____

_____

_____

_____

_____

_____

_____

_____

_____

_____

_____

_____

_____

_____

_____

_____

_____

_____

___5. Check your paragraph for errors in grammar, spelling and punctuation. Underline the topic sentence (and clincher if you've used one), number the specifics, and write "Ex" before each extender sentence.

Check the Answer Key on p. 176 before continuing.

• EXERCISE E

Plan and write a paragraph developed by *an incident*. Follow these steps, checking them off as you go.

___1. Choose one of the following subjects or a similar one assigned or approved by your instructor:
   a) Problems of Substitute Teachers
   b) Cost of Dates—Who Should Pay?
   c) Taking (or Giving) Advice
   d) Worry—A Useless Activity
   e) My Father's Method of Punishment
   f) Borrowing or Lending
   g) Taking a Dare

___2. Using the following chart, plan your paragraph. Write a general statement about your subject in the space provided. Think of *an incident*—a brief story of something that happened to you or someone you know—that illustrates or proves the general statement. In the appropriate blanks, write the different parts of the incident—the separate events, steps, or various important details that develop your story.

GS _____

_____

SP _____

SP _____

SP _____

SP _____

_____3. Check your specifics to make sure you have included all important parts of the incident, but that you have not included anything that does not develop your story.

_____4. In the space provided below, write the paragraph. Be sure to provide enough explanation about the various parts of the incident (in extenders) so that the reader does not have to fill in the gaps.

——5. Check your paragraph for errors in grammar, spelling and punctuation. Underline the topic sentence (and clincher if you've used one), number the specifics, and write "Ex" before each extender sentence. (In a paragraph developed with an incident, it is often difficult to distinguish SP's from EX's; therefore, do not worry needlessly if you have trouble separating the two kinds of sentences.)

Check the Answer Key on p. 176 before continuing.

• EXERCISE F

Plan and write a paragraph developed by *reasons*. Follow these steps, checking them off as you go.

——1. Choose one of the following subjects or a similar one assigned or approved by your instructor:
   a) Being (Having) an Only Child
   b) The Need for Solar Heating
   c) Should One Always Tell the Truth?
   d) Early Marriage vs. Late Marriage
   e) Early Choice of a Career

——2. Using the chart below, plan your paragraph. Write a general statement of your opinion on the subject in the space provided. List specific *reasons* that support your general statement. If you have difficulty thinking of reasons, read the topic sentence to yourself and then ask the question, "Why?"

GS _____

_____

SP _____

SP _____

SP _____

SP _____

——3. After you have listed your reasons, check them to make sure that all are directly related to the topic sentence. Eliminate any that are not, and add any new ones that occur to you.

_____4. In the space provided below, write the paragraph. You will probably need to explain each reason with several extender sentences.

_____

_____

_____

_____

_____

_____

_____

_____

_____

_____

_____

_____

_____

_____

_____

_____

_____

_____

_____

_____

_____

_____5. Check your paragraph for errors in grammar, punctuation and spelling. Then underline the topic sentence (and clincher, if there is one), number the reasons as they appear in the paragraph, and write "Ex" in front of each extender sentence.

Check the Answer Key on p. 176 before continuing.

STEP 17

Selecting Types and Combinations of Specifics

Not every paragraph you write will be limited to a single type of specifics. You may need to use two or more types—say, facts plus examples—in order to develop the topic sentence adequately. The writer determines the type(s) of specifics to use by looking at the topic sentence and asking, "What type or types of specifics will best explain or support this general idea?"

• EXERCISE

Imagine that the general statements listed below are topic sentences of paragraphs. After each one write the type or types of specifics that you think would best support that topic sentence.

1. My life is based on certain principles and I attempt to live by them each day.
   Type(s) of Specifics _____

2. While in many ways I am eager to be independent, there are some decisions that I would rather not have to make for myself.
   Type(s) of Specifics _____

3. If I were head of this school, I would make some radical changes.
   Type(s) of Specifics _____

4. I simply cannot stand people who think they know everything.
   Type(s) of Specifics _____

5. It is really quite simple to change a tire once one knows how.
   Type(s) of Specifics _____

6. As strange as it may sound, I have learned many things about myself by reading books.
   Type(s) of Specifics _____

7. Volunteerism succeeds most fully where the least economic sacrifice is required.
   Type(s) of Specifics _____

8. There seems to be no such thing as total satisfaction this side of the grave.
    Type(s) of Specifics ⎯⎯⎯⎯⎯⎯⎯⎯⎯⎯⎯⎯⎯⎯⎯⎯⎯⎯⎯

9. The Grand Canyon was the most beautiful spot we visited on our vacation.
    Type(s) of Specifics ⎯⎯⎯⎯⎯⎯⎯⎯⎯⎯⎯⎯⎯⎯⎯⎯⎯⎯⎯

10. What does it mean to be a "good citizen?"
    Type(s) of Specifics ⎯⎯⎯⎯⎯⎯⎯⎯⎯⎯⎯⎯⎯⎯⎯⎯⎯⎯⎯

11. Gasoline conservation is essential if we are to continue driving our cars in the next decade.
    Type(s) of Specifics ⎯⎯⎯⎯⎯⎯⎯⎯⎯⎯⎯⎯⎯⎯⎯⎯⎯⎯⎯

12. The telephone is a great boon to a shy person.
    Type(s) of Specifics ⎯⎯⎯⎯⎯⎯⎯⎯⎯⎯⎯⎯⎯⎯⎯⎯⎯⎯⎯

Check your answers on p. 176 before continuing.

Improving the Paragraph IV

STEP 18   Ordering Specifics

The reader will find your paragraph much easier to follow if you arrange your specific details in a logical order, rather than writing them down in whatever random way they first occur to you. Look over your list of specifics *before* you begin to write your paragraph and decide what is the most logical order of presentation. Some examples of the most important types of order follow.

Order of Time or Sequence.   The specifics listed below are listed in *time* order: from first to last, from beginning to end, from earliest to latest.

> GS   When I wash my car, I like to do it properly.
> > SP   First, I gather all the clean rags and sponges, soap, water and other equipment.
> > SP   Then, I make sure all windows are rolled up tight.
> > SP   Next, I proceed to wet and soap down all parts of the car.
> > SP   Then, I rinse the entire care very thoroughly.
> > SP   Finally, I dry it off with a chamois or soft cloth.

Order of Importance.   The specifics below build in *importance* from least to most important. It is equally possible to go from most to least; what is essential is that there be a definite pattern in one direction or the other.

63

GS Three qualities characterize a good citizen.
  SP Of course, every good citizen should be well informed about current events.
  SP In addition, a good citizen obeys all the laws and respects the government.
  SP But perhaps of greatest significance is the good citizen's willingness to use the right to vote and the right to participate fully in the governing process.

Order Necessary to Show Contrast or Comparison. When a general statement contains an obvious comparison, the supporting specifics may be ordered in one of two ways.

a) 1X, 2X, 3X, then 1Y, 2Y, 3Y
   This order is shown in the example below, where all specifics about dogs are placed first, followed by comparable specifics about cats, presented in the same order.

  GS Cats make better pets than dogs.
    SP Dogs are messy, do not clean up after themselves. (1X)
    SP Dogs eat too much food, require too much care. (2X)
    SP Dogs jump up on people, knock over furniture. (3X)
    SP Cats, on the other hand, are clean and tidy. (1Y)
    SP Cats eat sparingly, take care of themselves. (2Y)
    SP Cats are usually well mannered, behave themselves. (3Y)

b) 1X/1Y, 2X/2Y, 3X/3Y
   This second pattern for comparison arranges the two groups of specifics in alternation, as shown in the following example.

  GS Cats make better pets than dogs.
    SP Dogs are messy, do not clean up after themselves. (1X)
    SP Cats, on the other hand, are clean and tidy. (1Y)
    SP Dogs eat too much, require too much care. (2X)
    SP Cats, however, eat sparingly, take care of themselves. (2Y)
    SP Dogs jump up on people, knock over furniture. (3X)
    SP But cats are usually well mannered, behave themselves. (3Y)

• EXERCISE A

Identify which order of specifics was used to arrange the details in each of the paragraphs below: *Time, Importance,* or *Contrast.* If the order is Contrast, indicate whether it is type A or type B.

1.   Every student should learn to type because of the many advantages typing has over script. First, typing is much less fatiguing than writing, especially when one uses an electric typewriter. One can type for hours without fatigue, while steady writing for a time will soon tire one's hand. Second, no matter how tired a person becomes, the character of typed letters never changes. On the other hand, script will tend to become sloppy after long periods of writing. Next, typing is always legible with a minimum of effort. At times personal script is so poor that it is difficult, if not impossible to read. Legibility can contribute to an improved grade, since a teacher is more likely to give a low grade to a sloppily written paper than to a neat, typewritten one. Another advantage is speed. A good typist can type from forty to seventy words per minute, while the same person can write only about twenty to thirty words per minute by hand.

Order of Specifics _____

2.   Women are said to be more changeable than men, and there does seem to be some evidence that this is so. Certainly, when it comes to the men they fall in love with, women make radical shifts during a lifetime. The little girl is drawn to the boy who is nice to her, who is good at games but lets her play, too. Her hero chooses her to be on his team and takes her part when others tease. As she nears puberty, she appears to lose some of the good sense she has shown thus far and begins to moon over distant heroes, often those with unseemly haircuts and lifestyles to match. She never meets the one she yearns for, but remains faithful to his picture or to his music. Fortunately, as she enters the later years of adolescence, she becomes somewhat more practical. She at least chooses someone near at hand, someone, usually, whose life has been more like her own, and who looks forward to a future much like the one she hopes for. She may sometimes be enticed, to her sorrow, by broad shoulders and a handsome face, but she has had little experience to teach her less romantic standards. It is some years later that she learns to appreciate steadiness and strength and warmth of feeling. Life teaches her, finally, the kind of man to value.

Order of Specifics _____

3.   Women's fashions tend to change more rapidly and radically than men's. In the early 1900s, all women wore their skirts down to the ankle. Today, skirt length varies from floorlength to ten inches above the knee. Women's shoes have also gone through all sorts of changes in the last seventy years. For example, boots for women were very common around the turn of the century. Then, for years, they were not considered fashionable. Today there are back in style again in all colors, lengths, and materials. In fact, today's woman can wear all types of clothes—even slacks and shorts—on almost any occasion. While all of these changes

were taking place in women's fashions, men's clothing remained pretty much the same until a few years ago. In fact, most men still wear the traditional "suit"—jacket, shirt, tie, and slacks—though bright colors, patterns, and a variety in cut are now more common.

Order of Specifics _____

4.   In order to become a cheerleader, one must fulfill a number of requirements. Of course a cheerleader should be a good citizen and a responsible person, for she must set an example for the rest of the school by faithfully attending all of the games and pep rallies, as well as other school activities. Also importance is a girl's appearance. She must look her best at all times, not only because she is, thus, more attractive, but because she is the school's representative. The next requirement is essential: pep. Pep is an important quality in any good cheerleader because she must get the crowd into the spirit of the game. But pep must be accompanied by skill in executing the various jumps, leaps, cartwheels, arm motions, and other acrobatic feats needed in cheerleading. Unless the cheerleader has this skill, simply having pep will not be enough. Finally, one qualification tops the list: a good, loud voice.

Order of Specifics _____

5.   An electronic computer, while able to perform certain mathematical calculations more quickly than a person's brain, does not have the brain's complex structure. While a human brain consists of trillions upon trillions of nerve cells, a so-called "electronic brain" contains only about ten million electronic components. A human has the ability to create, to exercise initiative, to deduct, to reach conclusions, to doubt, to reason logically. A computer can only compute; it can multiply, divide, add, subtract, and perhaps extract roots. Also it must be carefully "programmed" in order to arrive at an answer; that is, it must be told in advance all the steps necessary to perform a particular operation. A human being, however, can be given a problem and can solve it with no further instruction. Most of the time taken up by a computer for problem solving is spent in locating the appropriate steps and intermediate values stored in its massive memory banks. The human brain, on the other hand, uses most of its time in actual computations. In short, a human brain is vastly more complex and versatile than a computer and is therefore far superior.

Order of Specifics _____

6.   No one should ever smoke in bed because the consequences can be drastic. My neighbor, Mrs. Smith, found this out the hard way a couple of weeks ago. Coming home late from work and feeling extremely tired, she fell onto the couch as soon as she entered her house. After an hour

or so, she got up the energy to fix herself some dinner. Then, still feeling weary, she took a warm bath and went to bed with a book. Soon afterward her troubles began. As she was reading, she lit a cigarette. Relaxed and comfortable, she began to doze over her book and, without realizing it, dropped her cigarette on the rug. A few minutes later she was fast asleep. Within an hour, smoke was rising from the rug, and moments later came the fire. When Mrs. Smith awoke, gasping for breath, she was horrified to find the floor in flames. Soon the fire department arrived and she was taken to the hospital suffering from smoke inhalation. Catastrophes like this would not happen so often if people did not smoke in bed.
Order of Specifics _____

7.   Racial disturbances are the result of many different problems. One cause is bad housing. Often, the only place a racial minority can live is in a tenement among rats and roaches. Trash and garbage litter the streets, and whole families are cramped into two or three rooms, sometimes without windows or plumbing. There are usually no recreational areas in these ghettos, and children are forced to play in the streets as a result. Living in this type of environment has helped lead blacks, chicanos and other minorities into revolt. In addition, unemployment is high among these groups because of job discrimination. When people cannot find work by which to support their families, they fall into despair and dissatisfaction and a riot is easily ignited. But perhaps the most significant problem is inadequate education. For example, the schools in many black communities lack equipment, facilities, and qualified teachers. Because of this, students often become apathetic about obtaining an education and drop out. Even interested students are not given the proper training required for life in our highly competitive society, and despite hard work they find it difficult to secure jobs and create a stable family life. Poor education, then, is at the heart of the problem, but it is accompanied by poor housing and unemployment. Only the elimination of these problems will lessen the threat of minority violence.
Order of Specifics _____

Check your answers on p. 176 before continuing.

In addition to the three main ways of ordering specifics—time, importance, contrast—there are several other logical orders which you may find useful.

Order of Familiarity. Moving from the known to the unknown, from what is familiar to the reader to what is less familiar.

Order of Complexity.   Moving from simple to complex, as in a series of examples or explanations or incidents.

Order of Agreement.   Starting with those parts of the topic with which the reader is likely to agree, and then moving on to the aspects that are more controversial or less likely to be accepted.

Order of Problem to Answer.   Starting with a discussion of the problem or conflcit, then moving to a presentation of the resolution or solution.

Order of Position.   Moving logically from one place or location to another, as in top to bottom, near to far, or left to right.

• EXERCISE B

Arrange the specifics in each list below in a logical order by numbering them 1, 2, 3, and so on. In the blank at the end of the list tell what order you used. You will probably use the three main orders—Time, Importance, Contrast—most often, but feel free to use any of the other five when they seem more suitable. If you choose order of Contrast, be sure to specify type A or type B.

1.   GS Education has a profound effect on development.

_____ SP Elementary school gives children an opportunity to develop basic skills, such as reading and writing, and to explore the natural world in which they live.

_____ SP The chief influence of college is the specialized training in a vocational field, as well as the much broader exposure to new ideas and attitudes.

_____ SP Nursery school or kindergarten usually provides children's first real chance to work and play with others their own age.

_____ SP In high school, the young people begin to understand themselves as unique individuals and to develop many new interests and ideas outside the family circle.

Order of Specifics _____

2.   GS Life in the city is considerably different from life in the suburbs.

_____ SP A person living in the city is close to many sources of entertainment.

_____ SP The streets of many suburban communities are lined with trees and shrubs and each house has its own grassy yard.

_____ SP People living in the city are constantly exposed to the hustle and bustle of urban life.

_____ SP If city dwellers want to see trees and grass, they must go to one of the public parks.

_____ SP Life in the suburbs is generally quiet and casual and generally more low-key than that in the city.

_____ SP Frequently, people living in suburban areas must go into the city for entertainment.

Order of Specifics _____

3. GS Watching the crowd at a baseball game is sometimes more interesting than watching the game itself.

_____ SP Down two rows and to the right is a row of twenty cans of beer, toward which a hand moves drunkenly, depositing the twenty-first empty besides the others.

_____ SP His rhythmic chant of "Peanuts, here!" rises and falls in measured cadence.

_____ SP Behind them, obviously amused at their unselfconscious lovemaking, is a spectacled old man, whose matronly wife is yelling vehemently: "Strike 'im out!"

_____ SP As one looks around the stadium, one witnesses a fascinating portrait of humanity in action.

_____ SP It totters on the edge of the wall and falls at the feet of the refreshment vendor.

_____ SP Farther down the row is a young couple necking passionately, oblivious to what is happening on the diamond.

Order of Specifics _____

4. GS Playing the guitar well requires knowledge of several skills.

_____ SP Learning the fingerboard is also an elementary step.

_____ SP After having mastered these three basic skills, one is ready to move on to a more difficult skill: learning the chord positions.

_____ SP Still another is memorizing the finger positions of the notes.

_____ SP The technique for holding the pick, although apparently unimportant, is actually basic to playing the instrument.

Order of Specifics _____

5. GS Canoeing in April becomes a wild adventure when showers make the rivers rise.

_____ SP We were lucky to reach our take-out point without suffering any serious mishap.

_____ SP Twice during the night we had to move the canoe to higher ground.

_____ SP When we put in, the canoeing was perfect, swift but not actually dangerous.

_____ SP The river was so high and wide we could not identify the channel but went where the white turbulence pushed us.

_____ SP It was barely sprinkling when we pitched our tent on a high bank.

_____ SP When water spilled over the sand bar's lip and put out our breakfast fire, we knew it was time to get down the river as quickly as possible.

Order of Specifics _____

6. GS It is next to impossible to make a wet basement dry.

_____ SP Other companies advertise basement waterproofing jobs that will not disturb either the exterior or the interior of the customer's house.

_____ SP In addition, window wells must be dug at least eighteen inches below window level and filled with gravel to allow for drainage.

_____ SP Even the tightest basement tends to ooze a bit when torrential rains put it to the test.

_____ SP However, the only sure method is to dig up the basement floor and lay drain tile to reduce hydrostatic pressure.

_____ SP Some paint companies claim to have a wall covering product which will not permit moisture to seep through.

Order of Specifics _____

Check your answers on p. 177 before continuing.

• EXERCISE C

Plan and write three paragraphs, using a different order or specifics for each. The orders, you will remember, are:

a) Time or sequence
b) Importance
c) Comparison or contrast (type A or type B)
d) Familiarity
e) Complexity

f) Agreement
g) Problem to answer
h) Position

Choose three different topics from the list below that will allow you to use different orders of details easily. Or use similar topics assigned or approved by your instructor.

a) The Unfairness of Some School Rules
b) How to Improve One's Vocabulary
c) Learning to Cook
d) Writing Letters
e) Giving a Successful Party
f) How to Become Wealthy
g) Freedom of the Press
h) Learning to Drive
i) If I Had Only Three Days to Live
j) How to Shop Wisely
k) Football versus Rugby (or Soccer)
l) Small Cars versus Larger Cars
m) Two Characters from Short Stories (Novels, Movies)
n) Why I Would (Would Not) Want to Live Forever
o) Life in the City versus Life on a Farm
p) Why Men Are Superior (Inferior) to Women
q) Styles in Clothing
r) Greatest Books of the Ages
s) How Movies Have Changed
t) Developing a Friendship
u) Training a Dog
v) The Life Cycle of a Tree
w) Ways to Increase Gas Mileage

Using the charts below, plan each of your three paragraphs as follows:

_____ 1. Write a general statement about the subject.

_____ 2. In the blank provided, write the type or types of specifics you think would be most appropriate for supporting the general statement.

_____ 3. List the specifics.

_____ 4. Decide what type of order the specifics should be presented in and write the type of order in the blank provided. Your choice should be made from the list above.

_____ 5. Number the specifics on the paragraph diagram so that you know in what order to present them in your paragraph.

_____ 6. Write the paragraph in the space provided, adding extenders as needed to explain the specifics.

Repeat these steps for Paragraphs 2 and 3, choosing topics that will allow you to use different types of orders for your specifics.

Paragraph #1

GS _____

_____

Type(s) of Specifics _____

SP _____

SP _____

SP _____

SP _____

Order of Specifics _____

Paragraph #2

GS _____

_____

Type(s) of Specifics _____

SP _____

SP _____

SP _____

SP _____

Order of Specifics _____

Paragraph #3

GS _____

_____

Type(s) of Specifics _____

SP _____

SP _____

SP _____

SP _____

Order of Specifics _____

Type(s) of Specifics _____

GS _____

_____

Type(s) of Specifics _____

    SP _____

    SP _____

    SP _____

    SP _____

Order of Specifics _____

_____

_____

_____

_____

_____

_____

_____

_____

_____

_____

_____

_____

_____

_____

_____

_____

_____

_____

_____

_____

_____

_____

_____

_____

_____

_____

_____

_____

_____

_____

_____

_____

_____

_____

_____

_____

_____

_____

Check the Answer Key on p. 177 before continuing.

Check the Answer Key on p. 177 before continuing.

STEP 19 — Adding Signal Words

You have learned previously that a good paragraph has *unity*; that is, it deals with only one topic—the one introduced in the topic sentence—and all specific details relate directly to this single topic. You have also learned that a good paragraph is *well developed*; that is, every general idea is supported with sufficient specific detail to make your ideas absolutely clear to the reader. Furthermore, you have learned that a good paragraph is *orderly*; that is, the ideas are presented in a logical pattern.

We now turn our attention to still another characteristic of a good paragraph: *coherence*. Coherence means, quite simply, "connectedness." The various parts of the paragraph stick together into a single entity, rather than a bewildering array of unrelated ideas.

One of the easiest ways to improve the coherence of a paragraph is to make liberal use of "signal words," special expressions that make clear the relationships among the ideas in the paragraph. These words can be thought of as giving the reader a signal as to what kind of idea is coming. For instance, if the next idea contradicts or modifies the previous one, an appropriate signal between them would be *but* or *however*. If the next idea is another in a series of reasons, a good signal would be *in addition* or *furthermore*. Such words help to explain the relationship between ideas and form a logical connection between specifics. They are essential to the clarity of your paragraphs. These signal words generally fall into six different categories:

Signals of Time and Sequence. Next, soon, then, later, finally, after, first, second, and so on, meanwhile, at length, in the past, in the meantime, afterward, after a few days, now, immediately, while, after a short time, thereupon, thereafter, presently, since, at last, of late.

Signals of Contrast. But, however, on the other hand, nevertheless, otherwise, yet, and yet, after all, at the same time, although true, in spite of, still, on the contrary, notwithstanding, in contrast, even so, for all that, while, nonetheless.

Signals of Listing and Adding. In addition, also, furthermore, moreover, another, likewise, similarly, next, finally, besides, first, second, (and so on,) again, the, and then, in the first place, too, equally important, and, further, last.

Signals of Results. Therefore, hence, thus, consequently, as a result, for, accordingly, thereupon, then truly.

Signals of Examples. For instance, an example of this, for example, take the case of, in other words, that is, as has been noted, in fact, specifically, in particular, indeed, incidentally.

Signals of Emphasis. Even, actually, as a matter of fact, surely, in fact, certainly, undoubtedly, indeed, true.

• EXERCISE A

Letter (a, b, c, and so on) the signal words sequentially as they appear in each of the following paragraphs. Then, in the appropriate space provided below, tell what *kind* of signal word each is: time, contrast, listing, results, examples, or emphasis.

1.   Being fat is not quite as bad as it seems. Cute overweight girls have more to admire when they look into mirrors. When they find a nice dress, there is more of it to look nice in. In addition, it is economical to be corpulent; because it costs the same for a size 18 as it does for a size 10, fat girls certainly get more for their money. Furthermore, a pleasingly plump lassie never has to be afraid of being called "Twiggy." Besides, in the case of a great famine as the result of the expanding population, tubby girls will live longer than thinner members of their sex. In old age, overweight girls will never have to find outside hobbies to fill up their time, for they will be constantly occupied with grocery shopping and letting out seams in their clothes. Finally, fat girls have one last fringe benefit: there is more of them for their boy friends to love. Therefore, don't count your calories, girls. Let it all hang out!

a) _____   d) _____

b) _____   e) _____

c) _____

2.   The mind is amazingly and maddeningly unmanageable. Who has not tried to pin his or her thoughts to some routine task, only to find them racing off like wild horses in some opposite and unplanned direction. At one moment, for example, I believe I am dutifully studying a dull but obligatory tract, eyes glued to the page, finger following down the text. See—I am turning the pages! But suddenly, for no apparent reason, I am aware that my thoughts are in my closet, planning tomorrow's wardrobe. Furthermore, I am aware that I cannot recall one word that I have been "reading" so studiously. Fifteen minutes have passed while I sat holding a book—hard working, responsible, bored. And what have I to show for my time? Nothing, since my coltish mind chose not to join me but to skitter off in other directions without my even knowing it until we rejoined one another in the closet.

a) _____   e) _____

b) _____   f) _____

c) _____   g) _____

d) _____   h) _____

3.   The habit of smoking is difficult to break. For one thing, the smoker is faced not only with a physical addiction to nicotine, but also to a series of behavioral habits of long standing. For instance, the smoker has become accustomed to lighting a cigarette when anything happens to cause stress. A phone call, a letter received, a visitor—all can be the occasion of some slight stress and, hence, of a cigarette. In addition, the smoker has gotten into the habit, very likely, of associating a cup of coffee with a cigarette. Coffee break, therefore, is cigarette break. The typical smoker also concludes each meal with a cigarette and, if he or she drinks, reaches for a cigarette to accompany each cocktail or highball. Such habits as these are hard to break. They become a part of unconscious daily behavior and exert a power far beyond that of physical addiction.

a) _____   e) _____

b) _____   f) _____

c) _____   g) _____

d) _____

4.   With regard to some aspects of life at least, the lower animals appear to be better served by their instincts than humans beings are by their impressive thinking capacity. For instance, animals always get the amount of sleep they need for good health. Human beings, however, put many other considerations ahead of sleep: watching television, reading a good book, making extra money—these are only a few on a long list of activities human beings consider more important than getting enough sleep. Human beings, also, consider many factors other than nutrition when they eat, whereas other animals, led by instinct, find and eat only those foods which nourish them. No normal animal below the human level would assault its system with the salty, greasy, high-calorie, non-nutritive snacks which do so much damage to the health of intelligent human beings. On the contrary, animals have built-in mechanisms which impel them to behave in ways supportive of optimum health and vigor. They do not seek danger in order to prove that they are brave. Nor do they fill their lives with ceaseless activity to prove how successful they can be. In short, the lower animals manage so well with their instincts that the highest animal might do well to ponder the benefits to be gained from imitating them.

a) _____   e) _____

b) _____   f) _____

c) _____   g) _____

d) _____

5. Human beings sometimes trivialize occasions of great consequence until their original significance is barely identifiable. Apparently, they hope thus to make occurrences of awesome magnitude into more easily manageable events. Americans have surely succeeded, for instance, with the Fourth of July, or Independence Day. True, the Stars and Stripes fly throughout the land, but the patriotic meaning of their presence is obscured in the clouds of firecracker smoke that fill the air. It is, indeed, likely that many American youngsters have never known or have forgotten entirely that the Fourth celebrates our Independence as a nation. Few adults seem inclined to remind them. Nor do many Americans appear to notice the incongruity of a Christmas celebration that gives a mere nod in the direction of the Star of Bethlehem before embarking on a protracted season of self indulgence and commercial frenzy. Santa Claus is, after all, a jolly old fellow, pleasant to have around and easy to understand. He is as popular, in fact, as the Easter Bunny, who appears in the Spring to help millions of people celebrate a religious event of unique splendor and significance. A basket of candy eggs, left in the night by a friendly rabbit, makes Easter real for many people. Most of us, as a matter of fact, are better able to deal with the trivial things of every day than with the great and abstract matters that tax our capacity to understand.

a) _____   e) _____

b) _____   f) _____

c) _____   g) _____

d) _____   h) _____

6. Occasionally, one meets someone who drinks a dozen or more cups of coffee in a day or who puts away a case of soft drinks within a twenty-four hour period. Assuming that such people eat three meals a day, do some kind of work, and sleep about eight hours at night, one wonders when they find time to partake of so much refreshment. But even more, once curiosity is aroused, one wonders what motivates them to do so. Thirst, the simplest and most logical motivation, is eliminated first. No human being in good health is thirsty at such brief intervals. A second motive, the desire to experience an exquisite taste, seems doubtful because other partakers of coffee or soft drinks fail to find them so alluring. Clearly, some people drink coffee or soft drinks with an enthusiasm that has little to do with taste. As a matter of fact, confirmed coffee drinkers will drink the dregs of a coffee pot when others cannot stand their taste. One wonders, then, if there is some bodily need, a craving of a physiological origin, which explains such frequent drinking, or, and this seems more likely, if it is not possible that these people are in the grip of a mechanical habit which has gradually taken such a hold on them that they go through the routine without even consciously deciding to do so.

a) _____   d) _____

b) _____   e) _____

c) _____   f) _____

Check your answers on p. 177 before continuing.

• EXERCISE B

Turn back to the paragraphs you wrote for Step 18, Exercise C. Insert any signal words you feel would help make the paragraphs clearer and easier to read.

• EXERCISE C

Write a paragraph according to the following steps, checking them off as you complete them.

_____ 1. Choose one of the following subjects or a similar one assigned or approved by your instructor:
   a) The Kind of Life I Want at Age Seventy-Five
   b) What To Do in Case of a Fire at Home
   c) Two Types of Smoke Detectors
   d) A Book (Movie) I Did Not Like
   e) Why I Like Sundays (Or Sundaes)
   f) The Nature of My Daydreams
   g) Salesclerks I Have Encountered

_____ 2. Using the chart below, plan your paragraph. First, write a general statement to serve as the topic sentence.

_____ 3. Then, list the specific details that support your general statement.

_____ 4. Make sure that all the specifics are directly related to the topic sentence. Eliminate any that are not; add any others that occur to you.

_____ 5. Decide on the most logical order for presenting the specifics. Write in the blank provided the kind of order you have chosen. (See Step 18.)

_____ 6. Number the specifics in the chart in the proper order.

_____ 7. Plan in your mind the extender sentences you may wish to use to explain each of your specifics.

_____ 8. Make note of any signal words that might be particularly helpful in making clear to the reader the relationships among your ideas.

GS _____

_____

SP _____

SP _____

SP _____

SP _____

Order of Specifics _____

_____ 9. In the space provided below, write the paragraph. You will probably need to explain each specific detail with several extender sentences; include at least one for each specific.

_____

_____

_____

_____

_____

_____

_____

_____

_____

_____

_____

_____

_____

_____

_____

_____

_____

_____

_____

_____

_____

_____

_____

_____

_____

_____ 10. Read your first draft to determine whether you have inserted signal words where needed. If you did not include them when writing the paragraph, add them now.

_____ 11. Check the paragraph for errors in grammar, punctuation and spelling. Then underline the topic sentence (and clincher, if there is one), number the specifics as they appear in the paragraph, write "Ex" in front of each extender sentence, and circle each signal word.

Check the Answer Key on p. 177 before continuing.

STEP 20   **Adding Other Connectors**

In addition to signal words, there are several other means of connecting the specifics in your paragraph. Here are three of the most useful.

1. Using pronouns which refer to words in preceding sentences. In the following example, "He" refers to "Terry" and "One" refers to "pencil." Such reference, through the use of a personal pronoun with antecedent in a preceding sentence, helps to tie the two sentences together.

> I handed a pencil to Terry, the boy who sits behind me in math class. He had forgotten to bring one and was desperate because the instructor had just announced a quiz.

2. Using demonstratives (this, that, those, these, such, and so forth) which refer to words or ideas in previous sentences. In the following example, "This" refers to the shyness that was described in the preceding sentence and helps to connect the two sentences.

> Bill Treadway had always been very shy. This shyness kept him from enjoying social activities.

Caution: avoid using "this" as a demonstrative pronoun with no definite antecedent:

> Bill Treadway had always been very shy. This kept him from enjoying social activities.

In this example, "this" has no definite antecedent in the preceding sentence. There is no noun for it to refer to, only an implied concept. An easy way to correct the problem is to change "this" from a demonstrative pronoun into a demonstrative *adjective* by inserting a word for it to modify (such as "shyness" in the first example above).

3. Using a word or phrase that has the same meaning or relates to the same thing as a word or phrase in a preceding sentence. In the following example, "The little devil" refers to "Chris" and thus helps to link the two sentences.

> My little brother Chris is a holy terror. The little devil is constantly in trouble at school and is almost impossible to live with at home.

• EXERCISE A

For each sentence given below you have a choice of two sentences which could follow it. Circle the letter of the one which is best connected to the first sentence. Look for the various types of connecting devices discussed above, as well as for signal words (Step 19). Underline the connector that caused you to make your choice.

1. I enjoy reading science fiction stories.
   a) *R is for Rocket* by Ray Bradbury was very exciting.
   b) For instance, I found Ray Bradbury's *R is for Rocket* very exciting.

2. Bill likes to travel very much.
   a) Perhaps Bill likes to travel because his father is an airplane pilot.
   b) Perhaps he likes it because his father is an airplane pilot.

3. Most women are sensible about how much make-up they use.
   a) But there are also those who think that the more they use, the better they look.
   b) There are some women who think that the more make-up they use, the better they look.

4. I forgot to bring the money for my bus ticket.
   a) I could not accompany my class on a field trip.
   b) Consequently, I could not accompany my class on a field trip.

5. Some people are so open and trusting that they discuss their personal problems quite willingly with friends.
   a) Others, however, are more reserved and maintain silence about personal matters, even with good friends.
   b) Therefore, others feel uncomfortable revealing any personal information to people outside their own family.

6. My mother's way of punishing me when I was a child was to make me stand in the corner.
   a) Ever since that time, I have had a deathly fear of corners.
   b) I am deathly afraid of corners.

7. It is not difficult to be the "life of the party." One method is to be up on all the latest gossip.
   a) It is always handy to know a lot of funny jokes.
   b) Another is to help keep the conversation lively and general enough to include everyone.

8. Autumn fruits and vegetables are particularly well suited to making a colorful centerpiece.
   a) One fruit that is especially vivid in an autumn arrangement is the golden delicious apple.
   b) The golden delicious apple makes a vivid show in an autumn centerpiece.

9. Breeding tropical fish is becoming a very popular hobby.
   a) It is a hobby enjoyed by adults and children alike.
   b) Children and adults both enjoy breeding tropical fish.

10. Young people are often advised by guidance counselors to choose a career before enrolling in college.
    a) But they do not always heed this advice.
    b) Young people do not always heed the advice of their counselors.

Check your answers on pp. 177–178 before continuing.

• EXERCISE B

Rewrite the second sentence in each pair below, providing any connecting devices and signal words that would improve the connection between the sentences. Underline your linking device in each sentence.

1. Franklin Prins was once a well-known attorney. Franklin Prins practiced law in my home town for thirty-five years.

   _____

   _____

   _____

2. When washing a dog, you should first fill a large tub with warm, soapy water. Find the dog and lure him into the tub.

   _____

   _____

   _____

3. In the novel, *Moby Dick,* Herman Melville uses many unusual devices to carry the story line through the book. Melville turns the novel into a play at several points.

   _____

   _____

   _____

4. In 1967, Great Britain devalued its unit of currency, the pound. Devaluing the pound had an effect on most of the countries in the Western World.

   _____

   _____

   _____

5. Choosing a career early in one's education has many advantages. An advantage of choosing a career early is that most of one's education can be planned with the chosen career in mind.

   _____

_____

_____

6. In my opinion, John F. Kennedy was a great President. One of the things that made John F. Kennedy a great President was that he inspired the youth of this country.

_____

_____

_____

7. Craig Breedlove had to risk danger in breaking the land speed record. Craig Breedlove had to place himself in a machine that could become a coffin traveling at 600 miles per hour at any moment.

_____

_____

_____

8. At Cyrano's customers are allowed to smoke anywhere in the restaurant. At the Chinese Castle patrons are asked not to smoke at all.

_____

_____

_____

9. My sister Suzanne is a fine dancer. She sings very well.

_____

_____

_____

10. The mayor was an ex-prize fighter who had been convicted of taking bribes. The mayor was not qualified for the position he held.

_____

_____

_____

11. In composing a good essay you should first plan and order each paragraph in outline form. You are ready to begin writing.

_____

_____

_____

Check the Answer Key on p. 178 before continuing.

• EXERCISE C

Write a paragraph following these steps and checking them off as you go.

_____ 1. Choose one of the following topics or a similar one assigned or approved by your instructor:
   a) Characteristics of a Memorable Person
   b) Causes of Marital Strife
   c) Weaknesses (Strengths) of the Jury System
   d) If I Became Wealthy Overnight
   e) America's First Ladies
   f) What Is Stress?
   g) My Favorite Relative
   h) Planning a Picnic
   i) Improving One's Will Power

_____ 2. Using the chart below, plan the paragraph. First, write a general statement about your subject to serve as a topic sentence.

   GS _____

   _____

   SP _____

   SP _____

   SP _____

   SP _____

   Type of Order _____

_____ 3. Then, list the supporting specifics.

_____ 4. Eliminate any unrelated specifics. Add new ones that occur to you.

_____ 5. Decide on the appropriate order for your specifics and write in the blank the type of order you have chosen.

_____ 6. Number the specifics in the proper order.

_____ 7. Plan in your mind the extenders you may wish to use to explain each of your specifics.

_____ 8. Make note of any signal words that might be particularly helpful in making clear to the reader the relationships among your ideas.

_____ 9. In the space provided below, write the paragraph. Explain each specific with one or more extenders.

_____

_____

_____

_____

_____

_____

_____

_____

_____

_____

_____

_____

_____

_____

_____

_____

_____

_____

_____

_____

_____

_____

_____

_____

_____

_____ 10. Read your first draft to determine whether you have inserted signal words and other connectors where needed. If you did not include them when writing the paragraph, add them now. In particular, be alert for opportunities to utilize the three types of connectors learned in this Step.

_____ 11. Check the paragraph for errors in grammar, punctuation, and spelling. Then underline the topic sentence (and clincher, if there is one), number the specifics as they appear in the paragraph, write "Ex" in front of each extender, and circle all the signal words and other connectors you used.

Check the Answer Key on p. 178 before continuing.

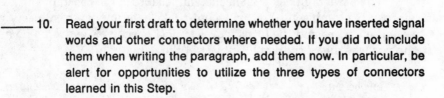

STEP 21
Achieving Coherence through Subject Consistency

Coherence, you will remember, means "connectedness," and is a quality that distinguishes good writing from that of less able writers. Signal words and other connecting devices are one means of enhancing the coherence in a paragraph. *Consistency* is another.

Two types of inconsistency can be particularly troublesome for beginning writers—shifts in subjects and shifts in verbs. The writer who begins writing from the point of view of third person plural (for example, people—they) and shifts in mid-sentence or mid-paragraph to the singular (a person—he) or even to the second person (you) or first person plural (we), needlessly confuses the reader. Similarly, shifts in tense or voice of verbs which are uncalled for by the sense of the passage being written create confusion. In this Step, you will learn how to avoid subject inconsistency; in Step 22, you will gain mastery over verb inconsistency.

To maintain subject consistency, choose the subject (in other words, the person or thing on which you wish to focus primary attention) and identify it in terms of person and number. Adhere to this point of view throughout the paragraph. Use this subject, or a synonym for it, or a pronoun referring to it as the grammatical subject of a sufficient number of sentences to establish it as the focus of your paragraph. A paragraph with a different grammatical subject in every sentence is very likely to be an incoherent one, unless some other means of achieving coherence is operating very successfully.

The paragraph below is incoherent because of the constant shifts in grammatical subjects. You will note that there are seven subjects in seven sentences and the focus moves almost entirely away from "homemakers who diet," the actual subject of the paragraph.

Incoherent:
  Homemakers who diet must find their task of losing weight made more difficult by the preoccupation with food of many publications. Magazines are filled with advertisements of food products, which are usually pictured in luscious color. Articles on homemaking seldom fail to include long passages about creative cooking and attractive serving of meals. The delightful descriptions and illustrations must tempt even the most determined dieter. Newspapers frequently include a food section replete with recipes and pictures of the final product. Someone in the family should go through such sections and cut out mention of all foods except diet food. Dieting would be much easier if such temptations were eliminated.

Applying the principle of subject consistency can remove all incoherence from the above paragraph. Identification of the subject as "homemakers who diet" or "dieters" or "they" and use of these as subjects of sentences throughout the paragraph keep the focus where it belongs and make it unlikely that any reader would fail to understand exactly what the paragraph is about.

Coherent:
  Homemakers who diet must find their task of losing weight made more difficult by the preoccupation with food in many publications. They cannot open a magazine without seeing page after page of advertisements of food products, usually pictured in luscious color. If they turn to an article on homemaking, they will undoubtedly be undermined by long passages about creative cooking and attractive service of meals. No matter how determined they are, dieters can hardly avoid being shaken by the delightful descriptions and illustrations. If they avoid such obvious traps and turn to the newspaper, even there they will find a thick food section with enticing recipes and pictures of the final products. Perhaps dieters need the help of a family censor who could go through all reading matter and remove the tempting allusions to food. Then they might find their dieting much easier.

• EXERCISE A

Examine carefully each of the paragraphs identified below, which appears in an earlier part of this book. Identify the subject which the author establishes in the first sentence and determine to what extent the author has successfully managed to stick with that subject consistently throughout the paragraph.

> Paragraph on cats in Step 15 (page 00)
> Paragraph on parents in Step 15 (page 00)
> Paragraph on Joan's vacation in Step 15 (pages 00-00)
> Paragraph on school administrators in step 16 (page 00)
> Paragraph on women in Step 18 (pages 00-00)
> Paragraph on animals in Step 19 (pages 00-00)

• EXERCISE B

Make each of the following passages more coherent by improving the subject consistency (in other words, revise the passages the same way that the "homemakers" example above was improved). Check your revision of each passage by turning to the Answer Key before beginning the next passage.

1. A professional athlete sometimes becomes the public's darling for a season or more for reasons not easy to fathom. Unpredictably, fans might take pleasure in a particular way an athlete wears his hair. Unusually romantic or poignant circumstances of a personal nature sometimes endear a player to the fans.

_____

_____

_____

_____

_____

_____

_____

_____

_____

_____

_____

_____

_____

_____

Check the Answer Key on p. 178 before continuing.

2. Baseball players are accustomed to hazards that cause a number of injuries each season. Sliding into a pair of waiting spikes is something every player has to do sometime. A pitched ball comes in at a speed of up to 90 miles an hour, and some pitchers have a reputation for being willing to dust back a threatening batter.

_____

_____

_____

_____

_____

_____

_____

_____

_____

_____

Check the Answer Key on p. 178 before continuing.

3. Oranges are an important part of a complete diet. Apples are nutritious, but they do not have nearly as much vitamin C as oranges. Bananas are a good source of potassium, but so is the orange.

_____

_____

_____

_____

_____

_____

_____

_____

_____

_____

_____

_____

_____

_____

Check the Answer Key on p. 178 before continuing.

STEP 22 — Achieving Coherence through Verb Consistency

To assure that your writing has maximum coherence, you should avoid inconsistent shifts in verb tense (for example, from past to present) and voice (for example, from active voice to passive voice). Use passive voice only when you are sure it does not reduce logic, clarity or impact.

The passage below is rendered incoherent by lack of care in maintaining the proper tense of verbs and by awkward lapses into passive voice. Careful attention to each verb shows four verbs in present tense and three in the past tense. Five uses of passive voice elevate the recipients of action to the position of subjects and reduce the performers of action to the lowly position of objects of prepositions.

Incoherent:

   We are led into a maze of tunnels by our guide, who told us not to be alarmed. We are taken into a room, where he told us we are going to be interrogated by other guards and given new identification papers by them. We are so frightened by his words that we had to be reassured by him over and over.

Can you identify the four present tense verbs and three past tense verbs? Can you find the five instances of passive voice? By changing the verbs so that tense remains consistent and by changing the passive voice verbs to active voice, one can produce a much more coherent version of this paragraph. Choice of past tense throughout and consistent use of active voice guarantee that the reader will know exactly what the paragraph is about.

Coherent:

   The guide led us into a maze of tunnels and told us not to be alarmed. He took us into a room, where he told us that some other guards were going to interrogate us and give us new identification papers. His words frightened us so that he had to reassure us over and over.

• EXERCISE A

Examine again the paragraphs listed under Exercise A, Step 21 above. Determine how verb consistency contributes to the coherence of these paragraphs.

• EXERCISE B

In the following brief passages, see if you can improve coherence by making the verbs consistent in tense and voice. Check the Answer Key after completing each item.

1. The baby was given his finger food by his patient and watchful mother. It is promptly pitched to the floor by the baby and picked up by the mother. Again the baby is given food, and again it is pitched to the floor. The game continued, with food being given by the mother and being tossed to the floor by the gleeful baby. It is not easy to predict whether the playful tug of war will be won by the mother or by the baby.

_____

_____

_____

_____

_____

_____

_____

_____

_____

_____

_____

Check the Answer Key on pp. 178–179 before continuing.

2. First, the incoming material which had to be catalogued and shelved was spread out on tables by the librarians. All the necessary information is noted and integrated into existing records, preparatory to the time when the new material would be offered by the librarians to the public. The task was accomplished in far less time than had been anticipated by the librarians.

_____

_____

_____

_____

_____

_____

_____

_____

_____

_____

_____

_____

_____

Check the Answer Key on p. 179 before continuing.

3. The garden, it was decided by the parents, would be planted that year by the children. Seeds were purchased by the children, accompanied and advised by the mother and father, and the day finally arrives when it is decided by the parents that the ground is ready. Seeds, tools, watering cans and hoses—all are carried by the children to the garden plot, where the hard work is begun. The vegetables are all planted in no time at all, and the rows marked by signs telling what had been planted in which rows.

_____

_____

_____

_____

_____

_____

_____

_____

_____

_____

_____

_____

Check the Answer Key on p. 179 before continuing.

STEP 23

Achieving Coherence through Completeness

Still another way of assuring that a paragraph is coherent is to give attention to *completeness*. Completeness in expressing one's sequence of thought is indispensable to coherence. Writers who leave gaps in their thinking, expecting their readers to fill in the gaps and infer the meaning not expressed, are asking more than is reasonable to expect of readers.

To achieve completeness in your writing, make explicit those steps in your thinking that are essential to the reader's complete understanding of your meaning. Here are two versions of the same paragraph, one with gaps in thought and the other more complete.

Incomplete:

Most family quarrels result from a failure of communication. If family members do not communicate closely, they will not have good understanding of one another. When family members drift apart, no one knows what others are thinking or what their needs might be. Quarrels are likely to ensue.

More complete:

Most family quarrels result from a failure of communication between family members. If family members do not communicate closely, they will not have good understanding of one another. It is common, when understanding is absent, to feel a lack of tolerance for others' behavior, and quarrels often follow. When family members drift apart, no one knows what others are thinking or what their needs might be. When needs conflict and siblings and parents are not aware of the nature or intensity of one another's needs, each member tends to pursue his or her own needs to the exclusion of those of others. Quarrels are likely to ensue.

The first paragraph leaves it to the reader to infer how the consequences of failure of communication would cause quarrels. The second paragraph makes explicit the steps in the train of thought that were only implied in the first paragraph. There seems little doubt as to which of these paragraphs would more successfully convey the full meaning of the author.

• EXERCISE

In the following passages, see if you can improve coherence by filling in all gaps in the expression of ideas, in much the same way as the "quarrels" paragraph above was improved through completeness. Feel free to invent suitable details as needed. Write your revisions in the spaces provided below. Check the Answer Key after completing each item.

1. Many young women are planning careers which they hope will make them financially independent. They wish to make their own mark in the world while, at the same time, making a marriage which will be emotionally fulfilling. Many of them would like to have children, but they realize there are other options. They seem unaware that their plans might be somewhat threatening to the kind of young man they hope to marry.

_____

_____

_____

_____

_____

_____

_____

_____

_____

_____

_____

_____

Check the Answer Key on p. 179 before continuing.

2. The picnic was to be on Monday. That was the only really convenient day that week. It rained on Monday. Tuesday was out of the question. Wednesday was not much better, but the picnic was finally set for Wednesday afternoon. Everyone had a good time.

_____

_____

_____

_____

_____

_____

_____

_____

_____

_____

_____

_____

_____

_____

Check the Answer Key on p. 179 before continuing.

3. There were 203 people in the graduating class. Only 198 were present for commencement. There were five empty seats in the front row. People tried to determine who was absent by checking the alphabetical list on the program. This was not very helpful. The spectators had to wait and see which students did not appear to receive a diploma when their names were called.

_____

_____

_____

_____

_____

_____

_____

_____

_____

_____

_____

_____

_____

_____

_____

Check the Answer Key on p. 179 before continuing.

4. Teenage marriages face many obstacles. Among them are the problems which arise when an inexperienced and undereducated young man faces the need to make a living. Young people, unfortunately, are seldom prepared to recognize and cope with the problems of homemaking. As time passes, of course, the young couple will continue to mature, but, unfortunately, they may grow into very different, even incompatible, people.

_____

_____

_____

_____

_____

_____

_____

_____

_____

_____

_____

_____

_____

Check the Answer Key on pp. 179–180 before continuing.

STEP 24   Hiding the Skeleton

There is a temptation, when one is writing by a pattern such as the one suggested in this book, to fall into what amounts, almost, to a repetitious singsong. It is altogether too easy to let the *structure* of the paragraph take over from the *substance,* as if the bones of the skeleton were showing through the flesh. Following is an example of such a paragraph.

> There are four reasons why Thanksgiving is the favorite holiday of many American families. The first reason is that it is, actually, a nationwide legal holiday. This means that everyone gets off work to enjoy a long weekend. The second reason why everyone likes Thanksgiving is that the weekend is long enough to allow families to get together for a long visit. This is a particular pleasure for people who live too far away to visit at any other time. The third reason many people consider Thanksgiving to be one of the best holidays of the year is that it is a time when one can count on wonderful food. This is because turkeys and pumpkins and many fruits and vegetables are in abundant supply in the fall. The fourth and final reason why people like Thanksgiving is that the fall of the year is such a beautiful time that everyone feels in a holiday mood. This is because the weather is cooler and the frost is making the trees into a brilliant display. Thanksgiving is, indeed, a favorite holiday of many people.

This paragraph is so obvious an example of poor writing that the steps for correcting it are equally obvious:

1. Do not begin a paragraph (at least not very often) with "There are" and particularly not with "There are four reasons" or "There are three ways" or "There are four examples." You do not need to announce that you are going to present four reasons or ways or examples. In short, you do not need to announce the structure of your paragraph.

2. Do not begin sentences with "This" referring to an entire previous sequence rather than to a noun or other pronoun. (Of course, "This is a pleasure" could become "This holiday is a pleasure," and the "This" would thus be salvaged by a more acceptable usage.)

3. Do not repeat your topic idea four times, in each of your four SP's. Look for variety of expression and have faith in the intelligence of your reader.

4. Do not, in a brief and uncomplicated paragraph, repeat your topic sentence in practically the same words, as a clincher sentence at the end. Your reader does not need that much help remembering the generalization that the paragraph presents.

Can you identify how the "Thanksgiving" paragraph above violates each of these four guidelines? The paragraph below follows the same pattern but does not burden the reader by including the pattern in the substance.

Thanksgiving is a favorite holiday of many American families. It is, actually, a nationwide legal holiday that provides almost everyone with a long weekend off the job. The four-day holiday is just long enough to allow families to get together for a long visit. Many families are spread so far apart that such long holidays give them the only times they can visit one another. The fact that the families come together to celebrate with food is by no means the least of Thanksgiving's charms. The turkey, the pumpkin pies, the special fruits and vegetables so abundant in the fall, are all American favorites. The time of year itself is particularly appealing for a holiday. The summer heat is gone and the same nip of frost in the air that colors the leaves makes everyone feel energetic and ready for festivities.

• EXERCISE

Following is a paragraph overburdened by structure made too explicit. Observing the four rules above, rewrite it in the space provided below, in such a way that the structure no longer dominates the substance. Feel free to add whatever details you feel would develop this paragraph in a complete and appealing way.

There are four categories of pets which live very comfortably with American families. The first choice of most Americans is some kind of dog. This may be a lingering consequence of pioneer days, when no family was without a dog to help both in protection and procurement of food. The pet which is second in popularity in America is the cat. This is amazing to dog lovers, who seldom understand the affection which some people have for the independent and mysterious cat. The third category of pets who live in the home with Americans is birds. This includes both the large, impressive birds who reside alone in a big cage and the little songbirds who live happily by twos and threes in a small cage. The fourth and final category of pets is fish, which is growing in popularity. This may be a reflection of the fact that a colorful fish tank makes such a beautiful addition to a room yet requires so little maintenance. Almost every American family has a pet from one of these categories.

_____

_____

_____

_____

_____

_____

_____

_____

_____

_____

_____

_____

_____

_____

_____

_____

Check the Answer Key on p. 180 before continuing.

STEP 25   Proofreading the Paragraph

By now you have learned to plan and write a paragraph carefully so that it says what you mean clearly and completely. But the job of writing a good paragraph does not end there. One more very important step must be taken: checking for careless errors. You must examine what you have written to make sure it is the best you can do and to eliminate any mistakes you can spot. Two things are essential to good proofreading: checking to make sure that your ideas are clearly presented and checking closely for specific errors you may have missed.

First, read your paragraph aloud in order to hear how it sounds. Hearing your writing will help you find gaps in your thought, ideas that are not explained adequately, careless omission of words, and obvious errors in punctuation and grammar. If you are embarrassed at the thought of reading your own paper aloud, find a secluded spot, turn the radio up to drown out your mumbling, and read quietly to yourself. If you have no hesitation about reading aloud, it is often helpful to read to someone else—someone who can tell you if your paragraph "makes sense" and if you have any glaring mistakes.

Then, read (aloud or silently) the paper through again several times—looking for a different type of error with each reading. Except perhaps for those persons who are trained in professional proofreading, it is not humanly possible to spot every type of error you may have made by reading your paragraph only once. You must read it a number of times in order to catch them all. Here is a list of the most common types of errors.

Poor Organization. Do you have a good topic sentence with supporting specifics? Do you need a clincher sentence at the end?

Weak Development. Is the topic sentence adequately supported with specifics? Have you provided extender sentences for all your specifics?

Unrelated Specifics. Do all of the specific details help explain or prove the topic sentence (that is, does the paragraph have unity)?

Poor Order of Specifics. Are your specifics arranged in some appropriate, logical pattern?

Incoherence. Have you been consistent in focusing on your subject throughout? Have you been consistent in the tense and voice of verbs? Have you filled in all the gaps in your thinking?

Signal Words. Have you provided the proper signal and linking expressions to connect your ideas?

Errors in Grammar. Are all your sentences complete? Have you improperly joined two sentences? Do subjects and verbs agree? Do pronouns and their antecedents agree? Are pronouns in the proper case?

Punctuation Errors. Have you used commas where needed to set off or separate items? Have you avoided using unnecessary commas? Have you used apostrophes correctly? Have you ben careful to use colons and semicolons properly? Have you avoided needless use of dashes?

Spelling Mistakes. Have you checked the dictionary for the exact spelling of any word of which you are not absolutely sure?

Neatness. Is your handwriting legible or your typing error free? Are your margins adequately wide and straight? Have you indented the first line of the paragraph?

After you have proofread your work, correcting errors and making improvements, recopy the paragraph before turning it in.

• EXERCISE

Proofread the paragraph below, which contains many of the errors outlined in this lesson. You should read the paragraph through once for each type of error. Correct the error in the paragraph itself by crossing it out and writing the correct form above it.

One who wishes to do some writing should first of all find a quiet well-lighted place with no detracting noises. The place they choose should have a level surface large enough for all the books, papers, and materials that they need. All these material's should be gathered before beginning to write. Since it is a waste of time to constantly have to stop and go running after a dictionary or thesaurus. The time one chooses to write is important. Generally it should be at a time convient to the author but it should not begin to late in the evening. Breaks in writing time is very necessary; since one cannot be expected to consentrate for long periods without a rest. In fact, research studys show that writers are more efficient if they write for about forty-five minutes and take a ten-minute snack break. One should be careful, though, that the "break" time does not exceed the amount of time sctually spent writing. Once the writer has found the proper environment for work and have established a time to begin, the real work starts. Writing is a complex process that requires consentration. If one has background material to read, the reading should be done actively; with an attempt to remember the points one plans to cover in the writing. Watching a serious television play also requires this same sort of active involvement. If one has taken notes which need to be reviewed, one should do more than skim over them half-heartedly. The practised writer will be thinking of possible situations to develop from these notes, by doing this, full use can be made of the material. Writers who take care to follow these steps when they write will find that the effort pays off in more and better writing for less effort.

Check your answers on p. 180 before continuing.

STEP 26   Trying It on Your Own

• EXERCISE

If you have worked all the steps preceding this one carefully, you will have learned how to write a good paragraph. Prove to yourself—and to your instructor—that you can do it by writing a paragraph on one of the topics listed below, or on one assigned or approved by your instructor. You should outline it on a separate sheet of ruled paper, according to the method you have learned before. Write a rough draft of the paragraph, proofread it, and then copy it over before submitting it to your instructor.

a) The Car I Would Like Most to Own
b) Decisions I Should Be Allowed to Make for Myself
c) The Fears I Live With
d) The Advantages (or Disadvantages) of Early Marriage
e) Two Different Teachers
f) The Causes of Family Quarrels
g) Learning from Failure

V
From Paragraph To Essay

Understanding the Essay

Perhaps while working in this book, you have said to yourself something like, "This paragraph is so long, it's like a whole essay." At that point you had an insight shared by all who write: the paragraph is, indeed, a composition in miniature. The paragraph and the essay, alike, make a comparatively general statement and develop it in detail.

The difference between the two lies in the size (the level of generality) of the idea being developed. The idea for the paragraph is small enough that it needs only to be developed by three or four supporting statements and extenders explaining or clarifying them. The idea for an essay, by contrast, is large enough that it needs to be divided into several parts and each of these parts then needs to be developed in at least one paragraph with several supporting statements and helpful extenders. Since each of the parts (main ideas of the essay) is then isolated in its own paragraph(s), the writer must preface them with a paragraph introducing and stating the overall idea of which they are the parts. With a conclusion following the developed paragraphs, the writer achieves a complete essay.

It is as if the structure of a paragraph were put under a photographic enlarger and expanded into a bigger version. Every element of the paragraph is in the essay—and in the same proportion.

Paragraph becomes Essay

Topic sentence   becomes   { Thesis sentence, included in opening paragraph

First supporting statement plus its extender(s)   becomes {
Topic sentence of first developed paragraph, with
1 SP + extender(s)
2 SP + extender(s)
3 SP + extender(s)
4 SP + extender(s)*

Second supporting statement plus its extender(s)   becomes {
Topic sentence of second developed paragraph, with
1 SP + extender(s)
2 SP + extender(s)
3 SP + extender(s)
4 SP + extender(s)

Third supporting statement plus its extender(s)   becomes {
Topic sentence of third developed paragraph, with
1 SP + extender(s)
2 SP + extender(s)
3 SP + extender(s)
4 SP + exiender(s)

Fourth supporting statement plus its extender(s)   becomes {
Topic sentence of fourth developed paragraph, with
1 SP + extender(s)
2 SP + extender(s)
3 SP + extender(s)
4 SP + extender(s)

Clincher sentence   becomes   { Concluding paragraph

To illustrate how a paragraph is an essay "in miniature" or, conversely, how an essay can be viewed as an enlargement of a paragraph, with all the same elements organized in the same way—just large in size, a paragraph that appeared previously in this book has been reproduced in the left-hand column below, with each of its elements clearly labeled. In the right-hand column is the outline for an essay on the same topic, with each of its elements matched with its counterpart in the paragraph. Notice how this example illustrates the diagram that appears on the previous page.

---

* Note: Not every paragraph, of course, will contain precisely four SP's with accompanying extenders.

PARAGRAPH	ESSAY
Topic sentence: The instincts of animals seem to enable them to preserve their health better than the vaunted intelligence of human beings.	*Introductory paragraph ending in thesis sentence:* When it comes to the preservation of health, animals seem to be better served by their instincts than human beings by their vaunted intelligence.

First supporting statement: When animals are sleepy, they find a quiet place and go to sleep. *Extender:* Human beings, on the other hand, often force themselves to stay awake and suffer afterwards from lack of sufficient rest.

Topic sentence of first developed paragraph: Wild animals show a great deal more wisdom than human beings, it would appear, in arranging the sleep they need for good health.

1 SP: Wild animals rest when tired.
    EX: Some by night, some by day
2 SP: When sun goes down, birds settle in.
    EX: When it comes up, they awaken.
3 SP: People largely ignore sun as clock.
    EX: Cannot make themselves go to bed or get up
4 SP: People put many interests before sleep.
    EX: Work, recreation, TV

Second supporting statement: Animals eat what is good for them. *Extender:* Most human beings eat many foods which add nothing to health or actually cause harm.

Topic sentence of second developed paragraph: Human beings would do well to imitate animals' tendency to eat what is good for them in amounts their bodies need.

1 SP: Wild animals, with instincts intact, know what to eat and what not and how much.
    EX: They know their natural foods, whether meat or vegetables.

2 SP: One does not see obesity among free animals.

EX: Amount of food fits activity and need.

3 SP: People eat too much, for wrong reasons.

EX: Eat from tension or depression

4 SP: People eat foods that harm their health.

EX: Eat salty snacks

Third supporting statement: Animals do not push themselves into a level of activity that exhausts them and threatens their health. *Extender:* Human beings often ignore their bodies' needs in driving themselves toward goals more important to them than good health.

Topic sentence of third developed paragraph: Human beings' intelligence tempts them into a routine of ambition and work that often undermines their health.

1 SP: Animals, driven by instinct, pursue only the work of survival.

EX: Feel no drive to change their environment

2 SP: Humans are unlimited in the aims and ambitions they can conceive and pursue.

EX: Once they imagine a goal, they drive themselves to achieve it.

3 SP: Animals therefore do not tax hearts and lungs beyond their capacity.

EX: Animals do not have ulcers and mental breakdown from overwork.

4 SP: Human beings even ruin health and life with work.

EX: Neglect families and joys of life

Fourth supporting statement: Animals, in the wisdom of their instincts, avoid danger.

Extender: People often fall into it or seek it for one reason or another.

Topic sentence of fourth developed paragraph: Human beings' brains sometimes seem to fail them when it comes to avoidance of danger.

1 SP: Animals instinctively recognize natural dangers and flee from them.

    EX: Antelope knows and flees from the tiger.

2 SP: Animals can sense a trap or difference in environment that might harm them.

    EX: They are aware of slightest change.

3 SP: An absent-minded person heads into danger totally unaware.

    EX: Our mind, busy elsewhere, works against us in such cases.

4 SP: Man even seeks danger.

    EX: For a thrill or to prove courage

Clincher: Perhaps if human beings could imitate the other animals, they would be healthier.

Concluding paragraph

• EXERCISE A

Read the essay below and mark it as follows.

1. Find the introductory paragraph and label it in the margin.
2. Place a wavy line under the thesis sentence.
3. Decide what three main supporting points are used to prove the thesis. Underline the topic sentences of the three paragraphs which explain each of these supporting points.
4. Examine each of the supporting paragraphs. Number the specifics which support the topic sentence and put a double line under the clincher, if there is one. Circle the signal words and connecting devices.
5. Find the conclusion and label it in the margin.

Joining the Peace Corps

The American Peace Corps, established during the administration of President John F. Kennedy, has proven once and for all that Americans will literally go to the ends of the earth to work for a better, more peaceful world. For little monetary return, but for the satisfaction of significant work and foreign travel, hundreds of thousands of American citizens have applied for an opportunity to serve abroad in the Peace Corps. Unfortunately, many applicants have had to be turned away. A great deal more than willing hands and an eager heart is required to perform successfully in the Corps. In order to be sure that the most qualified applicants are accepted, a complex procedure governing application has been set up. The applicant must meet certain qualifications, respond to questionnaires and examinations, and go through a period of training.

Applicants must have several qualifications. First, they must be at least eighteen years old and citizens of the United States. They can be married, but if a couple wants to serve, both partners must have suitable skills. A third qualification is vocational skill. This term means that applicants must already know how to do something, such as teaching or farming, because the program has no provision for training people in the skills that will later be imparted to others. Neither a college education nor prior knowledge of a foreign language is required, however. Another qualification is that applicants must not have any serious physical, mental or emotional disturbances. Most important of all, though, they must be willing to work hard for two years.

If their qualifications meet Peace Corps standards, applicants must provide various kinds of information. First, they must fill out a questionnaire, listing skills, hobbies, educational level achieved, schools attended, special interests, and work background, if any. Applicants must also provide references from friends, teachers, and/or employers. Furthermore, they must take placement tests—which are noncompetitive and test aptitudes and ability to learn foreign languages. A volunteer is picked for training on the basis of the information given on the questionnaire, the aptitude and ability shown on the tests, and references submitted.

After taking the tests, chosen volunteers must go through a training period of approximately twelve weeks, either at a United States training center or in the assigned country. During this time volunteers are taught a great deal about the country in which they will be working. They study its history and culture. They are also given technical, physical, and health training to enable them to remain healthy while living under conditions that are not always the most healthful. Another important part of the training is learning the language of the assigned country. A volunteer can expect at least 300 hours of language instruction. When the period of training ends, final selections of volunteers are made.

After the final selections, successful volunteers are sent to a foreign country for two years of service. By the time these two years are completed, they understand that the initial selection and training process was worthwhile.

Check your answers on p. 181 before continuing.

• EXERCISE B

The following essay is somewhat more complex than the first one you examined, but it has the same general structure. Read through the entire essay once, then go back and mark it as follows, checking off each step as you complete it.

_____ 1. Find the introductory paragraph and label it in the margin.

_____ 2. Place a wavy line under the thesis sentence. Be sure you have chosen the proper one. Remember: the thesis sentence is one sentence, contained in the introduction, which gives the central idea or opinion that the essay will try to prove.

_____ 3. Decide what three main supporting points are used to prove the thesis. Underline the topic sentences of the paragraphs which explain each of these supporting points.

_____ 4. Number the specifics in each paragraph which support the topic sentence. (Don't confuse explanatory and extending information with the main specifics.)

_____ 5. Draw a double line under the clincher, if there is one.

_____ 6. Circle the signal words and connecting devices throughout the essay.

_____ 7. Find the conclusion and label it in the margin.

Parent-Child Communication Problems

Today's teenagers encounter many problems in their diversified lives. Nevertheless, few teenagers ever discuss their worries with their parents—the two people who love them most and want the best for them—but prefer to talk about the problems with friends. Most adults feel they are aware of their teenager's problems and are readily available to help solve them. But teenagers often fail to bring their problems before their parents because they sense in them distrust, preoccupation, and a lack of understanding—all of which seem to be contributing factors in this unfortunate failure to communicate.

Many adolescents feel that an older person, such as a parent, is unable to relate to the problems of the present day youth. Some parents fail to understand because of different experiences and problems. For example, most parents see "going steady" as undesirable, even though most teenagers do it. The reason they dislike this practice is that when they were young it meant the couple was planning to be engaged soon. Now, of course, this is not the case. Other parents tend to underestimate the pressures on today's students, such as the necessity of getting superior grades in high school. When they were ready to go to college, the main requirement was having enough money. Today, however, it is necessary for students to be in the upper fifth of their class to be admitted to a competitive university. Such things may be extremely important to the teen, yet can seem merely foolish to an adult who does not realize the seriousness of the problem. Parents also fail to realize the change in life style their teenagers are making. They often cannot accept the fact that the dependent adolescent is changing into a self-reliant adult. Along with this change emerge added responsibilities and privileges. When giving advice, however, many parents act as though they were addressing a young child rather than someone who is almost an adult. Because of this lack of understanding on the parents' part, teenagers feel they have no choice but to turn to their friends, who have similar problems and are more apt to be understanding. Simple misunderstandings, then, such as those mentioned here, may become major stumbling blocks to attempts at communication between teenagers and parents.

Distrust is another cause of this lack of communication. While parents may say they trust their teenagers, their actions often indicate otherwise. For example, many parents listen in on their children's phone calls or open their mail, because they do not trust them to behave themselves properly. Also, parents frequently impose unreasonable restrictions on the activities of their teenaged children, simply because they do not trust their judgment. No young person is going to talk openly to an adult who shows no faith in the teen's intelligence or actions. Furthermore, many parents demonstrate quite clearly that they are not deserving of trust themselves. It may be that they simply repeat to another person in the family something told them in confidence, but to many teens this is an act of disloyalty. When this kind of mutual distrust develops, the lines of communication break down.

Another reason teenagers do not bring their problems to their parents is that the parents are often too busy or too wrapped up in their own lives to give them the attention they need. To some parents, social commitments are more important than being at home to discuss the problems of their children. Or they feel that they can fulfill their responsibilities by giving their children money and a car. Some fathers, for example, are so busy working to provide these material comforts for their families that they have no time left to spend with their children. Even the television set can become an obstacle between parents and children. It is next to impossible for teenagers to bring their problems before their parents when they are sitting glued to the screen all evening, every evening. Parents who are too involved with their own activities to notice their teenagers' problems force them to seek advice elsewhere. In such families, lack of communication is due to the parents' selfishness.

Lack of communication between the generations will continue until adults realize that teenagers are maturing individuals who need attention, understanding, and respectful trust. Lack of any of these elements in the parents' attitude will always create barriers between teenager and parent. These barriers must be broken and conquered before meaningful communication can begin.

Check your answers on p. 182 before continuing.

• EXERCISE C

Fill in the chart below by selecting the appropriate items from the essay above. You may abbreviate if necessary.

Thesis Sentence _____

_____

_____

First Main Point _____

    GS (Topic Sentence)_____

        _____

        SP _____

        SP _____

        SP _____

Second Main Point _____

    GS (Topic Sentence)_____

        _____

        SP _____

SP _____

SP _____

Third Main Point _____

    GS (Topic Sentence)_____

_____

SP _____

SP _____

SP _____

Check your answers on p. 183 before continuing.

STEP 28

Having an Idea about a Subject

The preceding section (Step 27) should have given you a clear understanding of the parts of an essay and their purposes. Now it is time to develop your ability to write an essay of your own.

Most essays that you will write, at least as long as you are still a student, are written in response to a topic assigned by someone else. Generally, an instructor gives you a subject or lets you choose a subject you are interested in—such as "motorcycles" or "decriminalization of marijuana" or "farming methods of Peruvian Indians." If you are lucky, you will be given a topic about which you know something or about which you care enough to learn about it. You are lucky, too, if the instructor lets you write on a subject of your own choosing.

But a good subject is only the beginning. Subjects are generally so very broad that no person could write about them with any amount of completeness. For example, millions of things can be said about motorcycles. The territory is too large to be covered by any one writer in any single essay.

Writing a good essay requires that you formulate an *idea* about the subject. The subject is the general topic that you will write about, whereas an *idea* indicates a specific focus or point of view toward that subject. The idea is what you can say *about* the subject. For example, "Motorcycles provide many Americans with an outlet for their aggressive impulses" is an idea *about* motorcycles. Here are other ideas about motorcycles:

> Since motorcycles cause so many injuries, they should not be available to the general public.
> Japanese motorcycles are greatly superior to their American-built counterparts.
> Driving a motorcycle can give one a sense of freedom that is difficult to experience in any other way.

Having an idea about a subject is not always as easy as it sounds—in fact, it is a process that most of us approach with equal parts of hope and trepidation. We hope an idea will come when we need one, but we are afraid that one will not. All too often, surely enough, an idea does refuse to dawn on us when we need it, and we are left hanging, as it were, not knowing how to make the stubborn idea come when it is called.

Fortunately, there is a technique for generating ideas which is very useful to writers and which is not difficult to learn. It simply requires the ability to relate two subjects not hitherto perceived to have been related. The result of such a deliberate and thoughtful combining is almost sure to be an idea. Following is a sample application of this technique. In the first column appears the subject assigned by the instructor or chosen by the student. In the second column is a second subject which the student arbitrarily pairs with the first. In the third column is the idea that can be formulated by relating the two subjects.

FIRST SUBJECT	SECOND SUBJECT	IDEA
Trees	Flowers	The presence of shade trees makes flower gardening a challenge.
Trees	People	Some people like trees.
Trees	History	The history of a place can be read in its trees.
Trees	Lawns	Where there are many trees, a good lawn cover like laurel or ajuga will be easier to maintain than grass.

• EXERCISE A

Following, on the left, is a list of subjects. Next to each subject is an idea about it. On the line to the right of each idea, name the second subject which was related to the first subject to produce the idea.

Example:

FIRST SUBJECT	SECOND SUBJECT	IDEA
War	civilians	In modern warfare civilians suffer as much as military personnel.

FIRST SUBJECT	SECOND SUBJECT	IDEA
1. Education	_____	The primary qualification for a trainer of dogs is patience.
2. Education	_____	Teaching as a career offers less job security now than in the past.
3. Education	_____	A national academy of the stature of West Point or Annapolis should be established to teach techniques for the waging of peace.
4. Health	_____	There is growing evidence that Americans eat far too much sugar for their health.
5. Health	_____	A zeal for profits has caused some employers to overlook or conceal threats to employees' health in the industrial environment.
6. Loneliness	_____	The need for acceptance into a group of

peers motivates much youthful behavior.

7. Spring   _____   The beauty of spring is all the more appreciated because it is delicate and ephemeral.

8. Baseball   _____   Big league baseball has become a multimillion dollar business which can afford to overlook the wishes of fans.

9. Feminism   _____   Writers who hope to publish their work will be wise to acquaint themselves with current interpretations of the term "sexist language."

10. Television   _____   Television commercials manage to convey the notion that to be old and look it is somehow obscene.

Check your answers on pp. 183–184 before continuing.

• EXERCISE B

On the lines provided below write whatever ideas you can derive by forming a relationship between the two subjects given. For example:

FIRST SUBJECT	SECOND SUBJECT	IDEA
Work	Happiness	The happiest people seem to be those who enjoy worthwhile work.

Try to express each idea in such a way that it could be used as the central idea (thesis) for an essay.

1. Education   Money

                _____

                _____

                _____

                _____

2. Education   Television

                _____

                _____

                _____

                _____

3. Education   Generation Gap

                _____

                _____

                _____

                _____

4. Health   Industry

                _____

                _____

                _____

                _____

5. Health   Babies

                _____

                _____

                _____

                _____

6. Loneliness   Self-awareness

                _____

                _____

                _____

                _____

7. Family Life   Crime

                _____

                _____

                _____

                _____

8. Autumn   Sadness   _____

_____

_____

_____

9. Art   Money   _____

_____

_____

_____

10. Sorrow   Joy   _____

_____

_____

_____

Check the Answer Key on p. 184 before continuing.

• EXERCISE C

Following are several general subject areas. Next to each, on the lines provided, try your hand at juxtaposing a second subject and formulating an idea that could be a thesis sentence for an essay.

FIRST SUBJECT	SECOND SUBJECT	IDEA
1. Cults	_____	_____
		_____
		_____
		_____
2. Daily Exercise	_____	_____
		_____
		_____
		_____

3. Anger   _____   _____

_____

_____

_____

4. Friendship   _____   _____

_____

_____

_____

Check the Answer Key on p. 184 before continuing.

STEP 29   Formulating a Thesis

Like the topic sentence in a paragraph, the thesis sentence in an essay is a general statement indicating what is going to be discussed. A good thesis sentence has the following characteristics:

1. It is a complete sentence (not, "Why running is good exercise," but, "Running is good exercise.").

2. It is general enough to incorporate all the specific details in the essay, but it is limited enough in scope to be developed in detail within an essay of the size assigned.

3. It is stated precisely, not vaguely or loosely, and the language is sufficiently qualified that the reader cannot mistake the exact dimensions of the idea being introduced (not, "Missouri is a great state," but, "Missouri's system of scenic waterways is second to none in the Midwest.")

4. It states the writer's opinion—the point of view or attitude toward the subject—rather than simply a personal preference or a statement of fact that requires no proof (not, "I like cats," or "Cats are feline," but "Cats also can be good friends.") In other words, a good thesis is, to some degree, arguable. Hence, "Flowers are pretty," is not as good a thesis as, "Flowers are more useful to science than most people realize."

• EXERCISE A

For each pair given below, circle the letter preceding the statement that is the better thesis for an essay of not over three or four pages. Keep in mind the requirements listed above.

1. a) There are fads in clothing.
    b) Clothing fads are often ridiculous.

2. a) The tricks used by advertisers to lure the public
    b) Advertisers use many tricks to get the public to buy their products.

3. a) The pros and cons of capital punishment are continually debated.
    b) Capital punishment should be abolished.

4. a) Winter sports are invigorating, interesting, and fun.
    b) Why people should participate in winter sports

5. a) A workable definition of "independence" is needed.
    b) What do we mean by "independence"?

6. a) The architect contributes much to modern America.
    b) The contribution of the architect to modern America

7. a) Senator Howard Anderson is attempting to have a law passed requiring every young person to spend two years in national service.
    b) Every young person should be required to spend two years in some form of national service.

8. a) I like friends who are loyal.
    b) Loyalty is an essential component of friendship.

9. a) Prudent teachers try not to require students to read books that offend the general standards of the community.
    b) Dirty books should be banned.

10. a) Everyone wants to get ahead in the world.
    b) Very little human behavior is entirely selfless.

11. a) I have always loved desserts too much.
    b) Not all desserts are fattening.

12. a) People of all ages have, throughout history, sought personal beauty in strange and sometimes destructive ways.
    b) Young people who have the most admired sun tans today may pay the highest price later in damage to their skin.

13. a) Peace is the highest aspiration in the world.
    b) The United Nations has made several significant contributions to the peace in Africa.

14. a) Too many young people smoke.
    b) Recent research indicates that moderate to heavy smoking accelerates the aging process, particularly in women.

15. a) Beauty, to a large extent, is a function of the nationality of the beholder.
    b) James Michener's book *Sayonara* gives a number of thought-provoking insights into Japanese standards for personal beauty.

16. a) The three branches of the federal government and how they balance
    b) The current balance of power among the three branches of the federal government is hardly the one envisioned by our founding fathers.

17. a) If national conventions are to be attracted to St. Louis, the downtown areas must have more cocktail lounges which offer nightclub entertainment.
    b) St. Louis night life does not offer much excitement to visiting sophisticates.

18. a) They had a wonderful time at Niagara Falls.
    b) Niagara Falls is a tourist attraction particularly well suited to honeymooners.

19. a) Those who did not receive awards were very critical of the awards procedure.
    b) A gracious loser demonstrates generosity of spirit and respect for himself or herself and others.

20. a) The capacity to accept the consequences of one's own behavior is the mark of a self-aware person.
    b) She blamed everyone but herself.

21. a) All the world loves a lover.
    b) People like to be around people who make them feel good.

22. a) The faculty committee expressed disapproval of his application for tenure.
    b) The most brilliant teachers and scholars on any college campus, in these days of fiscal retrenchment, are not necessarily those protected by tenure.

23. a) How to make superb Linguine Carbinara
    b) Linguine Carbinara is a superb pasta dish that can be made in less than a half hour when unexpected guests drop in for dinner.

24. a) One of the best things about Thanksgiving dinner is that the traditional menu can easily be prepared by a beginning cook.
    b) Thanksgiving recipes for the beginning cook

25. a) A growing number of young people each year are not planning to attend college.
    b) A good education will continue to give a young person an edge in the job market.

26. a) Who says you have to go to college?
    b) In a technological society such as ours, many young people who lack an academic bent would profit more from technical training than from a four-year liberal arts degree.

Check the Answer Key on pp. 184–185 before continuing.

• EXERCISE B

Look back at the statements of ideas that you wrote for Exercises B and C in Step 28. Revise each of them so that they meet the standards for thesis sentences listed earlier in this step.

STEP 30   **Organizing the Essay**

Once you have had an idea for your thesis and once you have stated it in precise and qualified language, you are in a position to know exactly what you must achieve in the body of your essay. At the very least, you must produce three or four paragraphs in which you develop in detailed language the various aspects of the idea presented in general language by your thesis sentence. And, of course, these paragraphs must be placed in an order which will contribute to the logic and clarity of your essay.

The nature of your thesis sentence, as well as its complexity and level of generality, will determine how you can best organize the body of your essay. Following are some patterns which may be useful in organizing different kinds of essays.

Example pattern. Suitable for a simple, indivisible thesis on a rather low level of generality, which can be satisfactorily specified by a combination of explanation and examples, this pattern is particularly useful for human interest features and articles. Following are three thesis sentences and outlines for essays based on them:

Thesis: The city council is usually composed of conversative people with records of solid achievement.
1. Introduction, including thesis sentence
2. Paragraph explaining why such people are needed on the council and/or are attracted to it
3. Paragraph presenting several brief examples of kinds of council members
4. Paragraph (or paragraphs) providing more extended example(s) as subject and assignment warrant
5. Conclusion

Thesis: A well planned border of perennial flowers can be a delight from early spring to late fall.
1. Introduction, including thesis sentence
2. Paragraph explaining the idea of a mixture of plants which bloom at different times but grow well together
3. Paragraph containing examples of plants for spring
4. Paragraph containing examples of plants for summer
5. Paragraph containing examples of plants for fall
6. Conclusion

Thesis: Children learn many important lessons when they are given responsibility for the care of pets.
1. Introduction, including thesis sentence
2. Paragraph containing brief examples of kinds of lessons learned
3. Paragraph containing more extended example of lesson, perhaps with regard to necessity of commitment
4. Paragraph containing climactic example of lesson, perhaps with regard to nature of death

Analysis pattern. For a complex thesis on a multi-faceted subject, one may organize as follows:
1. Divide the subject into its various facets.
2. For each facet, repeat the following pattern:
   a) Identify and explain or clarify the particular facet of the subject.
   b) As desirable, give examples or facts further developing the facet.
3. Arrange in logical order, following the principles suggested in Step 18.

Thesis: In every country overrun by the Nazis in World War II, resistance forces remained operative, providing a variety of services to the Allies at great cost to their own ranks.

1. Introduction, including thesis sentence
2. One or more paragraphs on the resistance movement in France
    a) Facts and figures on resistance
    b) Services rendered the Allies
    c) Degree of success and its cost to resistance
    (A separate paragraph could be devoted to each of the three aspects of French Resistance or all could be covered in one paragraph.)
3. One or more paragraphs on the resistance movement in Belgium
    a) Facts and figures on resistance
    b) Services rendered the Allies
    c) Degree of success and its cost to resistance.
    (Again, a separate paragraph could be devoted to each of the three aspects of Belgian resistance or all could be covered in one paragraph.)
4. Same pattern for other countries
5. Conclusion

Thesis: All three candidates have been evaluated in terms of their moral character, leadership ability and service to the organization.

1. Introduction, including thesis sentence
2. Paragraph on first candidate, discussing
    a) Character—description and examples
    b) Leadership—examples
    c) Service—examples
3. Repeat the same pattern for each of the other two candidates
4. Conclusion
    (Alternately, a complete paragraph could be devoted to each aspect of each candidate, rather than lumping character, leadership and service into a single paragraph for each candidate.)

Contrast pattern.   Suitable for a thesis which calls attention to differences between two or more subjects, this pattern is similar to that discussed in relation to the order of specifics in a paragraph of comparison/contrast (Step 18, page 63). If the essay is to be brief, with only one or two points of difference involved, the author may simply present one subject in its entirety and then the other, emphasizing the difference. If the differences are extensive, however, it is helpful to use the differences themselves as a framework for organizing the essay, as follows:

1. First difference (A and B)
2. Second difference (A and B)
3. Third difference (A and B)

and so on in logical order. Following is a sample thesis sentence and an outline of an essay organized according to the contrast pattern:

Thesis: The instincts of animals seem to enable them to preserve their health better than does the brain power of human beings.
1. Introduction, including thesis sentence
2. Paragraph discussing differences in arranging for sleep (first animals, then people)
3. Paragraph discussing differences in eating habits (first animals, then people)
4. Paragraph discussing differences in level of activity (first animals, then people)
5. Paragraph discussing avoiding danger (first animals, then people)
6. Conclusion

Comparison pattern. Suitable for a thesis which calls attention to similarities between two or more subjects, this pattern is most often used to clarify an unfamiliar or complex subject by likening it to a more familiar, simpler subject. As with the contrast pattern, it is usually best to use the similarities, not the subjects themselves, as the organizing structure:

1. First similarity (A and B)
2. Second similarity (A and B)
3. Third similarity (A and B)

and so on in logical order. Following is a sample thesis sentence and an outline of an essay organized according to the comparison pattern:

Thesis: Marlowe's journey up an unnamed African river, in Joseph Conrad's *Heart of Darkness,* is much like the journey through life every person must undergo.
1. Introduction, including thesis sentence

2. Paragraph discussing the need for work to structure one's days and years (first Conrad, then life)
3. Paragraph discussing need for commitment to a transcending value (first Conrad, then life)
4. Paragraph discussing the necessity for choice between good and evil (first Conrad, then life)
5. Paragraph discussing the necessity for giving up one's illusions (first Conrad, then life)
6. Paragraph discussing necessity to face death (first Conrad, then life)
7. Conclusion

Persuasion pattern. Suitable for a thesis that is so controversial that opposing arguments must be acknowledged and disposed of before the reader can be expected to accept the one being presented in the essay, this pattern—as its name implies—is used when the purpose of the essay is persuasive, rather than simply informative. If there is only one opposing argument, it can be stated and disposed of at the beginning of the essay and the remainder of the essay can be devoted to support of the thesis idea. If there are a number of opposing arguments, however, these may be used as a framework for organizing the essay, as follows:

1. First opposing argument stated and refuted
2. Second opposing argument stated and refuted, and so on, in climactic order, ending, perhaps, with a final paragraph (or more) presenting additional affirmative arguments for which no opposition needs to be acknowledged.

Here is an example of a thesis and outline for an essay organized according to this pattern:

Thesis: Student writers should be taught to plan carefully before writing an essay.
1. Introduction, including thesis sentence
2. Argument that planning destroys spontaneity—stated and refuted
3. Argument that planning takes the pleasure out of writing—stated and refuted
4. Argument that the best work comes from "free," unplanned writing—stated and refuted
5. Other arguments against the thesis stated and refuted in as many separate paragraphs as there are arguments
6. One or more paragraphs arguing in favor of careful planning by student writers
7. Conclusion

• EXERCISE

For each of the thesis sentences in the following list, choose the pattern of organization which you believe would be most suitable. Place the letter of the pattern you choose on the line to the left of each number. A = example, B = analysis, C = contrast, D = comparison, E = persuasion.

_____ 1. Parents should not be compelled by law to send their children to school.

_____ 2. The later works of William Butler Yeats bear little resemblance to the poetry he wrote as a young man.

_____ 3. One close and trusted friend is enough to provide the love and support that make troubled times bearable.

_____ 4. The new curriculum has the same weaknesses as the one teachers rejected several years ago.

_____ 5. If one wishes to succeed as a politician, there are four cardinal rules of behavior to observe.

_____ 6. Throughout human history, knowledge has imprisoned us as often as it has set us free.

_____ 7. Some first ladies have been more esteemed by the American public than their husbands have been.

_____ 8. Numerous medical authorities insist that running is a risky form of exercise for anyone over forty.

_____ 9. At least three powerful lobbying groups influence Congress to act contrary to the will of the American public as consistently expressed by polls.

_____ 10. The strategies used in football resemble those of war.

_____ 11. A critically acclaimed novel written in 1979 could never be mistaken for one equally well received in 1899.

Check your answers on p. 185 before continuing.

STEP 31   Preparing the Outline

Having formulated your thesis sentence and determined which pattern of organization is most suitable to develop it, you are ready to prepare your written outline as a guide for writing the essay. The outline should consist of:

1. Thesis sentence

2. Main points listed in a logical order (See Step 18; this information applies to the main points of the essay as well as to those of paragraph.)

3. Paragraph outline for each main point (Although you may find it appropriate to write more than one paragraph for each supporting point in some instances, the one point/one paragraph rule is helpful in the beginning.) Outline paragraphs as follows:
   a) Write a topic sentence (general statement).
   b) Decide on the best kinds of supporting specifics.
   c) List the specifics. Eliminate any not directly related to the topic sentence.
   d) Decide on the most logical ordering of specifics.
   e) Number specifics in the order in which they will appear in the paragraph.
   f) Add signal words where appropriate.

4. Any needed signal words at the beginning of paragraphs to help the reader see the relationships among your main points (paragraphs). Add them to your outline before beginning to write.

• EXERCISE

Demonstrate that you can apply these steps to your own writing. First, choose one of the following essay topics, or a similar one assigned or approved by your instructor:
a) Is Religion Dead in the Twentieth Century?
b) What It Means to Be Mature
c) The Changes I'd like to Make in Myself
d) Running
e) Exercise
f) Perfect Marriage
g) The Search for Inner Peace
h) The Perfect Community

Plan your essay by filling in the chart below. At this point you are simply to plan the essay. Do not write it in final form until you have worked through Step 32. Follow the steps given above in filling out the chart.

Thesis Sentence: _____

_____

_____

First Main Point: _____

    GS _____

    _____

        SP _____

        SP _____

        SP _____

        SP _____

        Order of Specifics _____

Second Main Point: _____

    GS _____

    _____

        SP _____

        SP _____

        SP _____

        SP _____

        Order of Specifics _____

Third Main Point: _____

    GS _____

    _____

        SP _____

        SP _____

        SP _____

        SP _____

        Order of Specifics _____

Continue for other main points.

Check the Answer Key on p. 185 before continuing.

STEP 32

Writing the Essay

• EXERCISE

Turn your outline (Step 31) into a complete essay as follows, checking each step off as you complete it.

_____ 1. Write an introductory paragraph containing the thesis sentence. Your first paragraph should provide an introduction to the central idea of your paper. Do not just plunge into your first main point. Instead, give the reader any necessary background information, explain why your topic is important, tell the reader what point you are setting out to prove (your thesis), and give the reader a clue as to how you plan to prove it. Not every introduction will include all of these things, but each must contain at least the thesis sentence. (See the introductory paragraph of "Parent-Child Communication Problems," page 113 for an example of a good introduction.)

_____ 2. Write a paragraph for each of the main supporting points, using as a guide the paragraph outlines you prepared as part of the essay outline for Step 31. Each of these supporting paragraphs should be organized in the same manner as the paragraphs you wrote in earlier lessons. (The introductory paragraph generally does not follow the standard pattern. It is a special purpose paragraph and has a pattern of its own which we will discuss in Step 33.)

_____ 3. Write a concluding paragraph to summarize your supporting ideas and give a sense of completeness to your essay.

_____ 4. After you have completed your essay, mark it as follows.
   a) Put a wavy line under the thesis sentence.
   b) Underline topic sentences of supporting paragraphs.
   c) Number the specifics in each supporting paragraph.
   d) Circle signal words in your paragraphs and those used to make connections between paragraphs.

   (Of course, these last four steps are simply to help you visualize the structure of your essay and usually would not be included in an essay turned in to your instructor, unless the instructor so requests.)

_____

_____

_____

_____

_____

_____

_____

_____

_____

_____

_____

_____

_____

_____

_____

_____

_____

_____

_____

_____

Check the Answer Key on p. 185 before continuing.

VI
Improving The Essay

Building Better Introductions

As was mentioned in Step 32, the introduction is a special purpose paragraph which orients readers to the topic and tells them what your are trying to prove. It should attract readers' attention and lead them into the essay. It often defines important terms, gives necessary background information, and previews the main points of the essay. And, of course, it *always* contains that *thesis sentence*—the statement of what it is the essay will attempt to prove. In this lesson we will look at three useful forms of the introduction.

Funnel Introduction. This is one of the simplest introductions, so named because it begins with a very broad general idea and continues with more and more specific ideas until it arrives at the thesis sentence— the most specific idea in the introductory paragraph. On the following page is an example of the *funnel* introduction, set up in the shape of a triangle to illustrate how it moves from the most general, through successively more specific ideas, to a statement of the thesis.

Notice how this introductory paragraph starts with a very general idea ("Why would anyone enter politics"). Then it moves to a more specific aspect of that idea (the "struggle with the obligations of public life") and, through three more sentences, to the even more specific statement ("their behavior must reflect those standards"). The final statement ("... there are three cardinal rules of behavior to observe if one wishes to succeed in politics") is the thesis and is the most specific sentence in the paragraph. (Again, remember that the introduction is a special kind of paragraph and does not follow the usual structure of general statement supported by specifics.)

Why would anyone enter politics? Why would anyone give up the ease of
private life to struggle with the obligations of public life? There
must be times when even politicians find it difficult to answer
these questions. But whatever the answer of each individual politician, the struggle—and the obligations—are
real. Politicians, once elected, are henceforth ob-
liged to consider the moral and social standards of those who elected them, and their
behavior must reflect those standards. In fact, one veteran Con-
gressman has said, there are
three cardinal rules of
behavior to observe
if one wishes to
succeed in
politics.

• EXERCISE A

In the space provided below try writing a funnel introduction to the essay you wrote for Step 32. Start with the most general idea you can think of that is related to your thesis. Compose sentences that are progressively more specific (at least two more steps) until you arrive at the thesis. (If you have trouble understanding how to write sentences that become progressively more specific, review Step 2.)

_____

_____

_____

_____

_____

_____

_____

_____

_____

_____

Check the Answer Key on p. 185 before continuing.

Contrast Introduction. The contrast introduction is another type of introduction that is easy to write, and it is especially appropriate when your thesis contradicts or modifies a commonly held belief or assumption. For example, if your thesis sentence is "It is more difficult to learn to ski than most people realize," you could write an introduction such as this.

> Most people assume that learning to ski is not extremely difficult. They imagine the process consists of little more than strapping on two long boards, pushing off at the top of a hill, and gliding gracefully and effortlessly to the bottom. Learning to ski is more difficult than these people realize, however, and requires long hours of practice, extremely good physical condition, and a lot of determination.

Notice that the *contrast* introduction starts off with a discussion of some commonly held belief or assumption. This assumption is explained in detail and then the thesis, the opposite of this assumption, is presented at the end of the introduction. Here is another example of the contrast introduction.

> *Ars longa, vita brevis.* (Art is long, life is short.) Thus, long ago, was expressed indirectly the artist's longing to produce somethng which would live beyond the human span of years, the longing to achieve immortality through art. Indeed, in ancient times it might have been easier for artists to believe that their works would be ageless. The record at that time was not long. In the 20th century, however, it is easier to perceive how very few are the artists whose works have been venerated across a span of centuries and how very, very many are the works, admired in their time, which are forgotten almost as quickly as the artists themselves. The dust bins of history are full of artistic works called great in their time which turned out to be merely stylish. (Thesis sentence underlined.)

• EXERCISE B

Using the thesis sentence you wrote for Step 32, write a contrast introduction similar to the examples given above. First, ask yourself what commonly held belief or idea your thesis contradicts. Start your introduction with a presentation of this assumption (perhaps beginning with the phrase "many persons assume. . ."), explain it in some detail (a couple of sentences), and then, after a signal of contradiction (*however, on the other hand, but*, and so forth), present your thesis. Write your introduction in the space provided below.

_____

_____

_____

_____

_____

_____

_____

_____

_____

_____

_____

Check the Answer Key on p. 186 before continuing.

Anecdotal Introduction. The anecdotal kind of introduction does exactly what its name suggests: it tells a story. The purpose of the brief story is twofold—to catch the reader's attention and to lead into the thesis sentence through an anecdote which illustrates it. Certain thesis ideas are "naturals" for this kind of opening paragraph, and that seems to be the case with the following example, which opens an article on how a beginning cook can succeed at cooking a traditional Thanksgiving dinner.

When Eleanor and Steve first became engaged, Eleanor was not quite nineteen, and Steve's grandmother was convinced that no eighteen-year-old could take care of her precious grandson the way he deserved. "Put her in a kitchen and she'd starve to death," Grandma muttered. But when Thanksgiving arrived, Eleanor proved her worth to Grandma beyond any doubt. She cooked the entire Thanksgiving dinner, from turkey through mince pie, for twenty relatives from the two families. Everything was delicious, and even Grandma found nothing to fault. Now, Eleanor was not exactly a beginning cook, but the lesson here is that even if she had been, she could still have turned the tables on Grandma. One of the best things about Thanksgiving dinner is that the traditional menu can easily be prepared by a beginning cook. (Thesis sentence underlined.)

• EXERCISE C

Using one of the subjects offered below, or a similar one assigned or approved by your instructor, formulate a thesis sentence, and then write an anecdotal introduction which will capture the attention of your reader and lead smoothly into your thesis sentence. Write your introduction in the space provided below.

a) A Painful Lesson
b) Procrastination
c) To Tell or Not To Tell
d) Conceit
e) Individuality
f) Self-Reliance
g) Patience
h) Courage

_____

_____

_____

_____

_____

_____

_____

_____

_____

_____

_____

_____

_____

_____

_____

Check the Answer Key on p. 186 before continuing.

Preview. A good introduction sometimes contains a *preview* of the main points that will be used to support the thesis. Such a preview is particularly helpful in a long essay based on the *analysis* pattern. The writer gives the readers a sort of "map of the landscape" or hint of the organization of the essay to make it easier for them to follow. The preview can come either before or after the thesis sentence and should be worked into the introduction in a way that avoids such obvious and awkward statements as "I shall prove this thesis by showing that. . . " Here is an introduction based on the *funnel* example above, but with a preview of the supporting points added.

> Why would anyone enter politics? Why would anyone given up the ease of private life to struggle with the obligations of public life? There must be time when even politicians find it difficult to answer these questions. But whatever the answer of each individual politician, the struggle—and the obligations—are real. Politicians, once elected, are henceforth obliged to consider the moral and social standards of those who elected them, and their behavior must reflect those standards. In fact, one veteran Congressman has said, there are three cardinal rules of behavior to observe if one wishes to succeed in politics. Politicians should marry young and stay married, upholding the sanctity of the home by spending as much time as possible in the bosom of the family. They should retain strong and active ties with the religion into which they were born, and, most helpful of all, politicians should spend as much time as possible associating with those who voted for them and demonstrating their appreciation of the roots from which their lives have grown.

You will remember that the thesis sentence is: "There are three cardinal rules of behavior to observe if one wishes to succeed in politics." Notice that following the thesis are listed three kinds of desirable behavior for politicians. These are the three main points, or *factors*, of the thesis, which will be used to support or develop it. Introducing them in the opening paragraph gives the reader a preview of how the paper will be organized. Given this preview, you would expect that the writer of the essay would devote at least one paragraph to family life, another (at least) to religious activities, and a third (at least) to the politician's need to maintain a close relationship with the voters who elected him or her.

• EXERCISE D

In each of the introductory paragraphs below, underline the thesis sentence. Then indicate in the blank which construction (*funnel, contrast,* or *anecdotal*) was used. Finally, number the *factors* in the *preview* of main supporting points, if a preview is included.

1.   Victory, oh, how sweet! How beautiful the words that name the victor, how welcome the applause, the spoils, the feeling of having overcome. It is natural at such a moment to be filled with generous feelings, to be moved to gracious behavior and comments. One rises to the moment. However, it is also easy at such a moment to forget that victory for one spells defeat for another, that what is glory on the one hand is gall on the other. It is then, at that moment when all is lost, that the nature of the loser of truly tested. It is then, when bitterness and spite might be expected, that the one who rises above mean and petty behavior is truly worthy of admiration. The gracious loser impresses all who observe by demonstrating generosity of spirit and respect both for self and others.
Type of Introduction _____

2.   "Look at what you made me do." The self-serving complaint of the small child is hardly different from the words with which adults disclaim responsibility for actions for which they do not wish to be blamed. "It was the other department that made the error." "It was a technical failure." "She shouldn't have repeated what I said." How easy and how natural it seems to be to rid ourselves of guilt by shifting the burden to someone else. And how few are those people who are able to say, with no apparent strain, "Yes, it was my mistake. I was wrong." Yet, how great would be the benefits to human society if this reflexive defensiveness could be overcome, so that people could be open with one another, and so that change would no longer be perceived as an attack on all that has been achieved in the past.
Type of Introduction _____

3.   When I was a teenager and having friends was one of the most important things in the world, I had a friend named Thelma. Of all the girls in our crowd, she was by far the most popular with both girls and boys. I was a little jealous, to tell the truth, and more than a little puzzled as to the secret of her popularity, since she was neither pretty nor talented. One night I discovered her secret. I was selling chances at a party and was immobilized behind a table so that all I could do was watch. I watched Thelma most of all because she was my friend and because she was always in the midst of a crowd. I watched her listening with a smile when someone talked to her; I saw her sit down by a newcomer who was alone; and I saw her sit, quiet and appreciative, when someone else had the floor. In short, I watched her long enough to learn why she had so many friends: People like to be around people who made them feel good.
Type of Introduction _____

4. California youth, those golden boys and girls from the land of constant sunshine, are setting America's standards for personal beauty these days. The sunbleached hair and sun browned skin are emulated, as much as possible, by young people—and many not so young—all over the country. The browner the better, insist those in search of beauty, ignoring the warnings of physicians about the harm which the sun's rays can cause to overexposed skin. Brown is in; brown is admired. It is regrettable that young people who have the most admired sun tans today may pay the highest price later in damage to their skin.

    Type of Introduction _____

5. Beauty, it has been said, is in the eye of the beholder. And where else could it be, one muses, since there are so many and such divergent views of what is and is not beautiful. The beholders are, of course, diverse in both an individual and national—or cultural—sense, and it is not surprising, therefore, that different cultures should have different standards of personal beauty. One finds it easy to agree with James Michener in a theme he expresses in more than one of his novels: beauty is to a large extent a function of the nationality of the beholder. In his book *Sayonara* Michener pays significant attention to this theme and in so doing offers a number of thought-provoking insights into Japanese perceptions of personal beauty.

    Type of Introduction _____

6. It occurred to me recently that I had not seen one of my daughter's friends for several weeks. "Jean," I asked, "where is that pretty little girl you used to walk to school with? Dorothy, I think her name was." Jean hesitated a moment before answering as if not sure what to say. Finally she replied in a thoughtful voice, "I guess I won't be walking with her any more, Mom. I told her I couldn't be her friend if she went on taking candy and things when we stopped at stores together." We were both quiet for a while, and then Jean said, "I feel sad about it, but I feel right too." I gave her a quick hug, feeling proud and pleased that she could have learned so well at twelve a lesson some adults never learn: loyalty to principle must come before loyalty to those who would be our friends.

    Type of Introduction _____

7. College is a complex mixture of academic and extracurricular activities. Although the academic side is perhaps the most essential, extracurricular activities often give students important opportunities for developing a sense of responsibility and increasing their ability to work with others. Students can find such opportunities in an athletic program. Sports help young people stay physically fit, while at the same time making them more responsible and better able to function in a group.

    Type of Introduction _____

Check your answers on p. 186 before continuing.

STEP 34 Providing Transitions and Connections

Just as it is necessary to add signal words and connecting devices between the specifics in a paragraph, it is also necessary to provide them between the paragraphs in an essay. These links are basically of the same types as those found within paragraphs:

1. Signal words at the beginning of a paragraph to show its relationship to the preceding paragraph and/or to the thesis idea (see Step 19).
2. Pronouns which refer to nouns in the preceding paragraph.
3. Transition sentences to remind the reader what point in the over-all outline has been reached. This is particularly suitable in essays where a preview of the essay's structure has been given in the introductory paragraph.
4. Repetition of key words or ideas from the last sentence of the preceding paragraph.
5. Reference to the main idea in a preceding paragraph.

Devices such as these provide a transition, or smooth movement, from one paragraph to the next, helping to eliminate awkward and abrupt interruptions in the flow of ideas. In your essay outline, include any transitional devices you think are needed between paragraphs. Then, when you write the essay, you can readily supply them to keep your ideas moving smoothly.

• EXERCISE A

In each group below you are given a sentence that you are to imagine is the last sentence in a paragraph, and two sentences from which to choose the first sentence of the next paragraph. Circle the letter preceding the sentence in each group that provides the smoothest transition. Underline the transitional or connecting devices.

1. A simple misunderstanding, then, can become a major stumbling block to communication between husband and wife.
    a) Fear of anger and expressions of anger can contribute to failure of communication between husband and wife.
    b) Fear of anger and expressions of anger can also contribute to failure of communication between husband and wife.

2. This habit of marking major generalizations as they occur will help the reader grasp the author's ideas and, at the same time, prepare the book for easy review at a later time.
   a) It is helpful to number supporting points in each paragraph.
   b) Another mechanical aid to understanding an author's development is the habit of numbering the supporting points in each paragraph.

3. A perennial border planned in this manner will offer a variety of blooms throughout the growing season.
   a) At the same time, the advantages of an annual bed for providing cut flowers should not be overlooked.
   b) One should not overlook the advantages of an annual bed for providing cut flowers.

4. This preoccupation with the past reflects the emphasis in modern psychology on formation of behavior patterns during early childhood.
   a) Despite the obvious importance of the past, however, the sensitive reader sees a deeper meaning in the novel.
   b) The sensitive reader sees a deeper meaning in the novel.

5. The group leader who deliberately models such accepting, non-directive behavior is thus more likely to develop a satisfactory level of trust among the members of the group.
   a) The shy group members are more likely to gain enough courage to speak up.
   b) As a result of this trusting atmosphere in the group, the shy members are more likely to gain enough courage to speak up.

6. The third basic pattern is order of importance, a method of organization in which the details are placed in ascending or descending order, according to how important they are to the argument.
   a) Any two or three of these orders can appear in the same paragraph, but usually one predominates.
   b) Often two or three orders can appear in the same paragraph, but usually one predominates.

7. Thus, the populations of Africa accepted the domination of whites for many years, apparently without question or regret.
   a) They will, however, no longer accept such domination passively.
   b) Africans will no longer accept domination passively.

8. And finally, tie shoes give the foot more support and are therefore more healthful.
   a) Slip-on shoes, generally called "loafers," are more popular.
   b) Nevertheless, slip-on shoes, generally called "loafers," are more popular.

9. These Greek myths, therefore, have much in common with the Biblical story of the creation.
   a) Likewise, both Greek mythology and the Bible contain stories of a great flood in which all but a few people were destroyed.

b) The story of a great flood in which all but a few people were destroyed can be found in both Greek mythology and the Bible.

10. The materials were assembled and I was ready to begin work immediately.

 a) I attacked the Spanish translation, which I dreaded the most.

 b) First, I attacked the Spanish translation, which I dreaded the most.

11. Undeniably, the cost in lives was high, but the French Resistance could take pride in their contribution to the liberation of France.

 a) Denmark provided a haven for thousands of refugees and escapees.

 b) Having shown that French resistance forces led all others in providing help to the Allied armies, it must be acknowledged that tiny Denmark led all other nations in providing a haven for thousands of refugees and escapees.

12. Thus, three million dollars and ten player trades later, the Spurts were ready to make their pennant bid.

 a) The Spurts were by no means the only club whose strategies centered on the check book rather than the playing field. The Critters were not far behind.

 b) The Critters excelled more at check book strategy than playing field tactics.

Check your answers on pp. 186–187 before continuing.

• **EXERCISE B.**

Look over the essay you wrote in Step 32. Determine whether the ideas flow smoothly from one paragraph to the next. Are the relationships between the paragraphs made clear? Add any connecting devices that are needed.

STEP
35
Learning to Conclude

Some students consider the concluding paragraph to be the most troublesome in the essay. Writing a conclusion should not be difficult for you if you keep the following points in mind.

1. *Summary.* Your conclusion can be a summary of the main points of your essay (stated in different words, of course, than when they appeared earlier) along with a restatement of your thesis (again in

different words). Such a summary and/or restatement is hardly necessary in a brief, three-point essay. Too much unnecessary repetition in a short composition is boring at best and insulting to the reader's intelligence at worst. On the other hand, a long, analytical essay, one which deals with a somewhat difficult subject, or which includes complex and extended arguments, could well be summarized in the concluding paragraph. The following is an example of this type of conclusion. It was written for the same essay introduced by the introductory paragraph that appears in Step 33, Exercise D, number 2.

> Perhaps in some gigantic plan, mysterious beyond our understanding, humankind's defensiveness was decreed for a useful purpose, but it is difficult to perceive what that purpose might have been. When we see how relationships between people could be improved, how free each could be to feel and express concern for the other, we can only wish that we had been created differently. And when we envision the future humanity could create if it were freed from defending the past, we can only hope that somehow, some day, we will learn to free ourselves from this fettering behavior.

2. *Repetition of Key Word.* Your conclusion will be smoother if you relate it in some way to the last supporting paragraph by repeating an appropriate key word or idea. The following illustrates this kind of linking to the previous paragraph. It is a conclusion written for the same essay introduced by the introductory paragraph that appears in Step 33, Exercise D, number 1.

> When the loser in a contest shows such graceful acceptance of defeat and comports himself or herself with such sincere self respect, the defeat is diminished. In any significant sense, what one is witnessing is a victory.

3. *Relevance of Central Idea.* If your readers need to see the relevance of your central idea to their own lives or to the world in general, your conclusion might point this out. The following illustrates this type of conclusion. It was written for the essay introduced by the introductory paragraph that appears in Step 33, Exercise D, number 4.

> These numbers regarding cases of skin cancer may seem remote— mere statistics. But the fact is that the medical statistics of the future will include some of the sun-lovers of today who are exposing their skin to too much sun. Now is the time to avoid the tragedy of skin cancer in the future.

4. *Significance of the Thesis.* Sometimes the reader comes to the end of an essay asking, "So what?" In that case, the concluding

paragraph needs to clarify the significance of the thesis. The following illustrates this type of conclusion. It was written for the essay on beginning cooks and Thanksgiving dinner introduced by the sample introduction that appears on pages 140–141.

> The friends and relatives sit, groaning happily, sure they will never be hungry again. But they will be—probably for left-overs, by early supper time. It is the cook—the beginner—who has experienced a "fullness" that will not go away. She has learned the satisfaction of doing the work, offering the gift, and receiving the thanks that are parts of feeding those you love. She should be the most thankful of all.

5. *Upside-Down Funnel.* Try constructing a conclusion that is an "upside-down funnel"; that is, start with a restatement of the thesis and then enlarge the idea with statements that become more and more general to show the setting which gives the idea its significance. The following illustrates the "upside-down funnel" conclusion. It was written for the essay on artists' work that did not stand the test of time, which is the introductory paragraph that appears on page 139.

> The comfort of the grave spared most of these artists from a realization of times' betrayal. They went to rest content that they had joined the immortals, that their names would be known forever, wherever humanity gathered. But even if they had known the odds against them or suspected them, is it not doubtful that they would have changed the aspirations of their lives? What was to be lost, after all? Knowing, as do we all, the brevity of life, they did well to devote their talents to the hope of transcending time through art. That they failed surely renders their effort no less worthy.

6. *Extended Clincher.* If your essay is short and you sense that a conclusion would sound "tacked on," solve the problem by writing an extended clincher for the last supporting paragraph, instead of composing an entire concluding paragraph. In this extended clincher you should "echo" the thesis statement. Imagine that the passage below concludes the essay on how to succeed in politics for which you have already read the introductory paragraph (page 142). You will remember that the third main point in that essay is the politician's need to maintain a close relationship with the voters who elected him or her. Imagine that the following passage appears at the end of the last supporting paragraph, in which this third main point is presented.

> . . . If the politicians stay close to those who trusted them enough to elect them in the first place, it is likely that they will remain in office for many years and will find their work much more a pleasure than an obligation.

• EXERCISE

Look again at the essay you wrote for Step 32. In the space provided below write a better conclusion for it by following some of the suggestions listed above.

_____

_____

_____

_____

_____

_____

_____

_____

_____

_____

_____

_____

_____

_____

_____

_____

_____

_____

_____

_____

Check the Answer Key on p. 187 before continuing.

STEP 36   Choosing Words Carefully

The words one chooses to express an idea convey, in addition to their literal meaning, many other feelings, impressions and attitudes. Imagine, for example, that a young man receives a serious cut in a street fight and appears at a hospital emergency room for treatment. The physician who examines him may later dictate a note such as the following for the patient's medical records: "This twenty-two year old white male presents with a severe laceration of the upper left. . . ." But the receptionist who saw him when he staggered up to the admitting desk might later tell a friend, "This guy walked up to me with blood just gushing out of his shoulder and said he needed to see a doctor. . . ." Which of these expressions conveys the idea correctly? Both of them, certainly. But each was "correct" for a particular purpose, at a particular time, and for a particular audience. We obviously vary the way we express an idea according to the situation.

In making choices about the way you will express ideas you will necessarily have to consider the purpose and audience you are writing for. Sometimes, like the doctor dictating a medical report, you will need to be extremely formal. At other times, like the receptionist talking to her friend, you can be breezy and informal. Generally speaking, though, the level of language chosen for any piece of writing is somewhat higher (that is, more formal) than the level of language used when speaking. It is not, therefore, good practice to "just write as if you were talking." Spoken English contains many features, such as incomplete sentences, that are rarely appropriate in written English. The good writer is aware of this difference and consciously selects the appropriate level of language for each composition.

In this section we will explore some of the problems in word choice that plague many beginning writers, most of which can be traced to difficulties in recognizing what kind of language is most appropriate for expressing ideas in writing.

The Indefinite "You."   The good writer attempts to achieve a satisfactory level of diction. The word "satisfactory" immediately leads one to ask "satisfactory to whom?" Is one writing to please oneself, to communicate with a dear friend, or to satisfy a demanding teacher or editor? If it is the latter—the teacher or editor—the writer would very likely use language and style of expression which resemble those of the paragraph being read at this moment. If, however, the writer is making an informal communication, the level of diction might resemble that of the following paragraph.

You alone can know the purpose for your writing. You know whether the second person "you" will be acceptable or whether you must be sure to use only third person, as in the preceding paragraph. If you find it comfortable to write using the general "you," there will be many occasions when that pronoun will be quite acceptable. If, on the other hand, you plan to write, say, literary criticism or an analytical treatise for your history professor, you will need to learn how to turn the second person into third person without destroying what you want to say. Let us see whether this paragraph that you are reading right now can be changed to one without the word "you."

The writer alone can know his or her purpose for the composition he or she is writing. He or she will know whether the second person "you" will be acceptable to his or her audience or whether he or she must be sure. . .

Now, there is a new awkwardness. When you (one) try (tries) to get rid of "you," you run into the problem of what pronoun to put in its place. With readers, editors and publishers newly conscious of the fact that "he"—for so many centuries accepted as the universal pronoun— leaves out half of the world, the writer has had to develop a new self- consciousness when he (or she) wishes to use third person, singular, in writing.

There are a number of ways to cope with this dilemma, all of which appear in this book from time to time. A partial list of techniques follows, but you would be well advised to talk with your instructor, or your editor if you are planning to publish a piece of writing, to discover whether the general "you" is acceptable and whether the pronoun "he" is acceptable to refer to all of humanity.

1. Choose a specific human subject and refer to him or her by the proper pronoun (Thelma—she).
2. Choose a plural subject and use "they," thus avoiding the issue of gender.
3. When the third person singular pronoun can be limited to one or two uses in a paragraph, use "he or she," "her or his," and "himself or herself," and so on. Obviously, continuous use of these forms in close juxtaposition becomes laughable, as we discovered in our attempt, several paragraphs earlier, to revise the paragraph containing "you."
4. Choose an impersonal subject which can be referred to by neuter pronouns. You may find yourself writing more about "writing" than "the writer," or "losing graciously" than "the gracious loser."

5. Change "you" to "one" (meaning "anyone") if the context does not require you to use "he or she" too frequently thereafter.

6. If you permit yourself the use of "you," be sure to avoid a use of that pronoun—which, after all, directly addresses the reader—which will bring a large segment of your readers (or your instructor) out of their seats, saying, "Who, me?!" If you address your reader as "you," you should be quite sure who he or she is going to be.

7. Some authorities on language usage have given their approval to the use of the third person plural pronoun to refer to such pronouns as everyone, everybody, anyone, everything, and so on, which are generally thought to be singular. Thus, according to these authorities, it is perfectly correct to write "Everyone picked up their briefcases and left to go to their jobs," eliminating the need to write, "Everyone picked up his or her briefcase and left to go to his or her job." Even though this usage is increasingly common in speech, it is not accepted by most instructors in writing, and it is best to avoid it.

• EXERCISE A.

It might prove useful to you, if you wish to avoid both "you" and the universal "he" in your writing, to look back through this book to observe the uses of the above techniques. Particular attention is called to paragraphs on pp. 66, 67, 79, 143.

• EXERCISE B.

The following brief passage uses the second person pronoun. On the lines provided, convert it to the use of the third person singular.

If you wake up in the night and smell smoke, you should immediately rouse other family members and get them out of the house. If, however, your access to other parts of the house is cut off, you should not delay, but should immediately get yourself out of the building and try to reach your family through other doors and windows.

_____

_____

_____

_____

_____

_____

_____

_____

_____

Check your answers on p. 187 before continuing.

• EXERCISE C

Convert the passage in Exercise B to the use of the third person plural.

_____

_____

_____

_____

_____

_____

_____

_____

Check your answers on p. 187 before continuing.

Contractions.   Another usage on which writers, teachers and editors sometimes disagree is the use of contractions. Generally speaking, a writing in which "you" is permitted might well also permit some use of contractions. More formal writing, however, is marred by the use of any but very infrequent contractions and even informal writing is made casual to a level of unattractive colloquialism by uncontrolled use of contractions for no reason other than habit. You would be well advised to eliminate all contractions if you are a victim of this habit. Remember: your reader cannot *hear* what you are writing.

• EXERCISE D

Read back through your writings so far and check your use of contractions. If you find that you habitually use contractions, begin changing that usage wherever you see it. Proofread the essay you wrote for Step 32 to be sure it includes no contractions.

Slang. The use of slang and markedly colloquial language is rarely, if ever considered satisfactory by those who teach or publish expository writing. While your writing should flow as naturally, directly and fluently as does your speech, it should at the same time be free of the intimacies, as it were, of speech: the slang words, the careless overuse of favorite words, elliptical statements, made-up words, lazy usage, and similar expressions.

• EXERCISE E

To the following brief list of slang expressions and colloquialisms, see how many more you can add out of your own personal experience.

snuck	cops	they could care less
guts	took the rap	out of his mind
groove on it	laid it on the line	terrific!
crazy	toe the line	knew her way around
kid	out of line	don't make waves
a phoney	go to pieces	rock the boat
fantastic!	all shook up	fit to be tied
guy	sure (for surely)	pretty (for quite or
horsing around	real (for really)	fairly)

• EXERCISE F

Read back through your writings so far to check for use of slang and other inappropriately informal expressions. Proofread the essay you wrote in Step 32. Does it contain instances of "underwriting"? Change any slang or unduly casual expressions you find to words or phrases that are better suited to writing.

Cliches and Stale Metaphors. As children we learn to write imitatively, and we believe that if our writing sounds like other writings we have read, we are successful. Only later do we learn that it is good to be original and try to express ourselves in fresh and lively ways. A beginning writer may feel entirely at ease using an expression such as "hard as nails" or "pretty as a picture." But as one gains more experience, one realizes that many comparisons have been used so many times that they are as stale as last week's donuts. As a rule of thumb, one can assume that if a comparison is familiar (that is, if one has seen it in print or heard it several times), it is well on its way to becoming trite and stale, and one would be well advised to avoid it. One can either replace it with an original comparison (one which the writer has not heard before but creates for the occasion), or—and probably much easier to accomplish—say precisely what one means without the use of metaphorical language (that is, instead of "pretty as a picture," try "extremely pretty").

• EXERCISE G

To the following brief list of cliches and stale metaphors, see how many more you can add out of your own personal experience.

last but not least	hot as a firecracker	snug as a bug in a rug
tried and true	ugly as a mud fence	diamond in the rough
hard as nails	slept like a log	cool as a cucumber
straight as a string	greedy as a pig	pleased as punch
dead as a doornail	ate like a horse	by leaps and bounds
quick as a wink	happy as a lark	regular as clockwork
sing like a bird	light as a feather	up in arms
slow as molasses in January	swore like a sailor	faster than greased lightning

• EXERCISE H

Read back through your writings so far to check for such cliches and metaphors as those listed in Exercise G above. Try to replace any you find with more precise expressions of your meaning or fresh comparisons. Then proofread the essay you wrote in Step 32 to make sure it does not contain such dull and imitative usage.

Overwriting.   As we discussed previously in this Step, some beginning writers make the mistake of choosing language that is too informal for the occasion. We sometimes call this error "underwriting." Other writers are guilty of just the opposite—*overwriting,* use of language that is on a level too high for the occasion. What leads writers to fill their work with "fancy" language? Perhaps it is because when we are children our teachers work to help us extend our vocabularies. They try to help us learn bigger, better words and more formal, complex constructions. Often students interpret these efforts to mean it is desirable to use "fancy" (formal, complex) language to express their thoughts in language as high brow and pretentious as they can possibly make it. This kind of writing is almost worse than the slangy, cliche-ridden kind, perhaps because it tends to convey a pompous sort of self satisfaction that is irritating to the reader. Good writers avoid "fancy" language and attempt to say exactly what they mean, as clearly and simply and precisely as possible.

• EXERCISE I

Rewrite the following brief and overblown passages in more precise, less pretentious language.

1. The gentleman whose candidacy is to be considered initially is one whose countenance has long been familiar to all who have participated in political activities in this enlightened municipality. His admirable intellectual capacities and elevated moral attributes provide grounds for the unshakable conviction that his would be a singularly productive contribution to the efforts of this governing body.

    _____

    _____

    _____

    _____

    _____

    _____

    _____

2. The second individual whose candidacy should occupy our attention is a virtual paragon of female virtues. Her achievements in response to a myriad of vocational and philanthropic challenges have been the subject of widespread expressions of praise by those who have been fortunate enough to have the privilege of becoming acquainted with her. Seldom have such a predilection for laborious effort and an unvarying demonstration of equanimity been so fortuitously united in one individual.

    _____

    _____

    _____

    _____

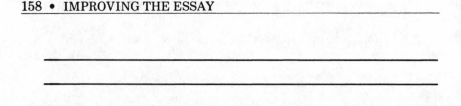

Check the Answer Key on p. 187 before continuing.

Redundant and Padded Writing. Sometimes, in the sincerity of our effort to convey our exact meaning to our readers, we feel the urge to say again, in different words, what we have already said. Given such a richness of choices in the English language to say any one thing, we sometimes cannot resist two or three ways and put them *all* in, hoping with such a shotgun approach to be sure to hit our target.

Of course, if you are saying the second time in more *specific* language what you have previously said in only *general* terms, you are properly performing the author's task. But if you are merely repeating yourself, in language that occurs to you as being somehow clearer or more attractive, then you should examine your motives as well as your words and eliminate the redundancy or repetition.

Sometimes, also, the use of one adjective or of one verb seems naked and incomplete and we are impelled to add a second, so that our adjectives and verbs go yoked in pairs and we wastefully use two words where one would do quite well.

Sometimes the rhythm of a sentence is, indeed, improved by adding a second adjective or verb—or whatever—but in such cases you should choose a word which contributes an additional nuance of meaning, so that its presence is justified. "Leaping and bounding" do not accomplish in tandem as much as do "leaping and tumbling," and "decorous and well behaved" do not reveal a polite young man nearly as well as do "decorous and eager to please."

Strive to be both efficient and economical in your use of words. Let each word be chosen so thoughtfully that fewer words suffice, for padding deadens your writing and unfairly steals the time of your reader.

• EXERCISE K

Rewrite the following redundant and padded passage to eliminate all words and phrases that say the same thing twice.

One must be thankful and full of gratitude for the privilege of being fortunate enough to know Mrs. Brown personally as an individual. Her charm and grace of manner are such that each and every one of her campaign workers reveres and venerates her in a manner not often observed in the attitude displayed toward such a young woman. Her youth belies her experience, however, as she has had as much experience as if she were older. Her constant and unending labors on behalf of the mayor's office for the past several years have brought her much appreciation for her continuous faithful service. And with all the praise she has received, she has remained modest and unassuming, with no desire whatsoever to boast and make much of her own accomplishments, according to the consensus of opinion among the associates who know her and colleagues who work with her.

_____

_____

_____

_____

_____

_____

_____

_____

_____

_____

Check the Answer Key on p. 187 before continuing.

• EXERCISE L

Read back through your writings so far to check for examples of both overwriting and redundant and padded writing. Give particular attention to the essay you wrote in Step 32 to make sure it contains no "fancy" language or redundancies and padding.

Unduly Metaphorical Language.   Sometimes, when they are having difficulty writing *precisely* what they mean, writers turn to metaphorical expressions which are similar in meaning to what they wish to say. In short, instead of saying what they mean, they say something else that means what they mean. For example, they may write "come to the end of the line" when they really mean "reach a point where no further alternatives are available." Or they may write "It was a mess," instead of the more precise "The situation was awkward and embarrassing for all who were involved." Or a writer might rely on an expression such as, "He was out of line," to convey "He behaved inappropriately," or "turned their backs on her" to mean "refused to associate with her" or "refused to respond to her needs." In so doing, the writers place on their readers the task of translating the metaphorical language into the precise meaning that is not expressed. This practice reflects a misapprehension of the tasks of the writer and the reader and is very unlikely to produce a complete understanding by the reader of the writer's exact meaning.

It is certainly a fact that an occasional imaginative and carefully selected metaphor enlivens writing and enlarges on meaning, but this fact does not justify seeking refuge in imprecise metaphorical language to escape the difficult obligation of conveying a precise meaning.

• EXERCISE M

Rewrite the following passage which demonstrates imprecise and unduly metaphorical language so that a more exact meaning is conveyed.

The group usually operated on a fairly even keel, although some of the lesser lights did, when the chips were down, feel as if they were being put down and crowded out of the limelight in an unfair manner. As a consequence, it was necessary to pull up short once in a while and clear the air so that no one felt left out in the cold. The moderator tried to lend a hand as best she could, but when all was said and done, she was a frail reed to lean on and it was the group members themselves who were forced to carry the burden.

_____

_____

_____

_____

_____

_____

_____

_____

_____

_____

Check the Answer Key on p. 188 before continuing.

• EXERCISE N

The following paragraph contains several types of problems in word choice and level of language. Revise it, attempting to make it as clear and precise as possible.

When he finally took his nose out of his work to take a breather, he walked over and looked out the window. Much to his surprise he noticed two guys yelling and cussing at each other in a real vulgar way. Pretty soon, before he could figure out what was what, this cop came pounding down the street yelling at the top of his lungs at these guys and waving his stick like crazy. Well, it was clear as a bell that these two guys knew when to knock it off and get lost. They took off in opposite directions like a couple of jackrabbits, leaving the cop all shook up, with no notion what the score was.

Check the Answer Key on p. 188 before continuing.

STEP 37 Proofreading the Essay

Your essay is not finished until you have proofread it carefully, corrected your errors, and recopied it. Proofreading an essay is exactly like proofreading a paragraph (see Step 25), but for the sake of clarity, let us review the process.

Read the entire essay aloud in order to hear what it sounds like. Listen for gaps in your thoughts, ideas that are not explained adequately, careless omission of words, and obvious mistakes in punctuation and grammar. You might also ask someone else to listen to you or to read the essay as well, looking for mistakes you have missed and making suggestions for improvement. Then read the paper through again several times—looking closely for a different type of error with each reading. Here are the most important types to watch out for.

Poor Organization. Does your paper have a precise central idea (thesis) stated in the introduction? Are the supporting points of this thesis given in logical order? Does your paragraphing indicate these logical divisions?

Weak Development. Is the thesis adequately supported with main points, each of which is developed in one or more paragraphs? Is the topic sentence of every paragraph adequately supported with specifics? Have you provided extender sentences for all your specifics within paragraphs?

Unrelated Specifics. Do all the main points relate directly to the thesis? Do all specifics in each paragraph help to prove or explain the topic sentence?

Lack of Order. Are the main points arranged in an appropriate, logical pattern? Are the specifics within each paragraph arranged in a logical order?

Incoherence. Have you been consistent in point of view? Are tenses consistent? Is passive voice avoided? Is the same grammatical subject used in most sentences within a particular paragraph? Are all gaps in thought eliminated?

Signal Words and Connectors. Have you provided the proper signal words and linking devices to connect paragraphs, as well as to connect the specifics within each paragraph?

Errors in Grammar. Are all your sentences complete? Have you improperly joined two sentences? Do subjects and verbs agree? Do pronouns and their antecedents agree? Are pronouns in the proper case?

Punctuation Errors. Have you used commas where needed to set off or separate items? Have you avoided using unnecessary commas? Have you used apostrophes correctly? Have you been careful to use colons and semicolons properly? Have you avoided needless use of dashes?

Spelling Mistakes. Have you checked the dictionary for the exact spelling of any words you are not absolutely sure of?

Neatness. Is your handwriting legible or your typing error free? Are your margins adequately wide and straight? Have you indented the first line of each paragraph?

• EXERCISE A

Proofread the essay below, which contains many of the errors outlined above. You should read the essay through once for each type of error. Correct the errors in the essay itself by crossing them out and writing the correct form above.

Cars I Would Not Want to Own

There are over a quarter of a million automobiles sold in the United States each year. Many types are available; foreign cars and American cars, convertables and sedans, big cars and little cars. This variety is the result of the wide range of tastes of the driving population. There is three kinds of cars which doesn't suit my taste at all, and which I would never own. One type is impractical, another is little and ugly, and a third is poorly made.

An example of an impractical car is the Excalibur SS, perhaps you have never seen one of these cars. It bears a strong resemblance to the Dusenberg of years ago or to an old MG, early 1951 or 1952. One of the things I don't like about it are that it only comes in a convertable model. That's fine in the summer or on a sunny day, but when it rains or when winter comes, its rather impractical. Winter is perhaps the roughest though. Mainly because the car is not even equipped with a heater. And the softtop has plastic side windows and a plastic rear window that leaks and yellows in the sun and becomes briddle with age. This car is fitted with a 327 cubic inch engine from the Corvette Stingray. The car does not weigh more than 2000 pounds, compared to the Corvette, which weighs approximately 3200 pounds this year. With over

350 horsepower and so little weight, the Excalibur is very dangerous, you can't come near controlling it on accelleration around curves or on a panic stop. Combining these shortcommings with a $10,000 price tag, you have a very impractical car.

A car that I wouldn't want is one of those ugly little foreign "bugs" you see everywhere. The Volkswagen is a good example, this simply isn't my idea of a car with good looks. In addition, its too small for safety. If you were hit in the side by a large car or by a truck, you'd be finished. You also can't ride for great distances in comfort, because the engine is to noisy and the interior is cramped. Another shortcomming is that Volkswagen's are to common. I don't want a car that every mothers son has, and if you look around any large parking lot in this city, you are bound to see at least ten Volkswagen's. Besides being so common, this car is to underpowered for freeway driving. Its almost impossible to pass a car on the expressway at fifty-five miles per hour, if there is a stiff crosswind blowing, you would think you were on a roller coaster. This is both unpleasant and unsafe.

The third type of car that I wouldn't like to own is one that is cheaply made. Ford Mustangs fall into this class—my family owned one once, and before we got rid of it the muffler fell off at least five times. By the time we sold it six months later, there was rattles in every corner. Meanwhile, the paint had started peeling off, to say nothing of the first layer of chrome on the bumpers. To top it off, whenever the driver made a hard left turn, the door on the passenger's side would fly open. My uncle owns a Cougar, and it doesn't have these problems.

Although I consider myself to be a fairly reasonable person, who can understand that different people like different kinds of cars. I simply cannot understand why anybody would buy the cars I've described here. If their impractical, I don't want them. If their "buggy," forget it. And if their cheap, please leave it on the display floor; because I'm not interested.

Check your answers on p. 188–189 before continuing.

• EXERCISE B

Proofread the essay you wrote in Step 32, reading through once for each type of error listed in this lesson. Then recopy it, using the best introduction and conclusion you wrote, and turn it in to your instructor.

STEP 38   Writing a Complete Essay

• EXERCISE

Applying all the principles you have learned in previous steps, write an essay of approximately 500 words. Follow these steps, checking them off as you finish each one.

_____ 1. Choose one of the following topics (or a similar one assigned or approved by your instructor) and write a thesis sentence based on it. Be sure that your thesis is at least somewhat arguable or controversial and that it shows your opinion or position on the question. Be sure your language is precise and qualified, so that the exact dimensions of your thesis are evident.
   a) Is TV Violence Really Harmful to Children?
   b) Why Young People Take Drugs
   c) Should Teenagers Be Allowed to Smoke?
   d) Is Peace Possible?
   e) The Importance of Moral Courage
   f) The Perfect Mate
   g) Hang Gliding
   h) Backpacking
   i) Feminism

_____ 2. Jot down the main ideas that support your thesis. Think about your thesis; ask yourself "why?" Decide what ideas prove or explain it. Combine those which are similar. Eliminate any that are not directly related to or do not really support your argument. You should end up with three or four main supporting points. Decide what pattern of organization might be suitable for your essay and put your main parts in logical and appealing order, numbering them in sequence. (Review Step 30 if you need help with this process.)

_____ 3. Using the chart on page 167, draw up an outline.
   a) Write the thesis sentence in the space provided and list the main points in the proper blanks, making sure they are in the order on which you decided.
   b) Starting with the first main point, construct a paragraph outline for each paragraph as follows:
      (1) Write a general statement (topic sentence) to introduce the main point.

    (2) Decide what kinds of specifics you need to explain and support the topic sentence.

    (3) List the specifics.

    (4) Check to make sure that all specifics are directly related to the topic sentence. Eliminate any that are not. Add any new ones that occur to you.

    (5) Decide what order would be most logical for presenting the specifics. Write the order you plan to use in the blank provided.

    (6) Rearrange specifics by numbering them in the order they will appear.

    (7) Add signal words where necessary within each paragraph.

  c) Add to the outline any signal words that will be needed to connect the paragraphs.

_____ 4. Begin to write the essay, following the outline you have constructed.

  a) Write an introductory paragraph. It must be *funnel, contrast,* or *anecdotal* in construction—depending on which you consider most suitable. Make sure your thesis sentence appears in the introduction. You may *preview* the main points of your essay in the introduction if you feel it would be helpful to the reader.

  b) Write a paragraph for each of the supporting ponts. Make sure you explain each specific idea adequately and provide adequate connecting material, using all necessary signal words and connectors. Write a *clincher,* or summary sentence, for any paragraph that needs it.

  c) Supply any transitions that are needed between paragraphs (see Step 34).

  d) Write a conclusion, following the suggestions in Step 35.

_____ 5. Go back and doublecheck your work as follows:

  a) Place a wavy line under the thesis sentence. Underline the topic sentence and clincher in each of the supporting paragraphs.

  b) Number the specifics within these paragraphs and label the extenders.

  c) Label the introduction either funnel, contrast, or anecdotal. If you have previewed your main points in the introduction, number them in order of their appearance in the body of the essay.

  d) Circle all signal words and connecting devices, both within paragraphs and between paragraphs.

  e) Proofread the entire essay, according to the instructions in Step 37.

_____ 6. Recopy the essay, ignoring the underlining, numbers and circles and submit the final draft to your instructor.

Essay Outline

Thesis Sentence _____

_____

_____

_____

First main point _____

    GS (Topic Sentence) _____

    _____

    _____

       SP _____

       SP _____

       SP _____

       SP _____

       Order of Specifics _____

Second main point _____

    GS (Topic Sentence) _____

    _____

    _____

       SP _____

       SP _____

       SP _____

       SP _____

       Order of Specifics _____

Third main point _____

    GS (Topic Sentence) _____

    _____

    _____

       SP _____

       SP _____

SP _____

SP _____

Order of Specifics _____

And so on for additional main points

STEP 39   Trying It on Your Own

• EXERCISE

Having worked through all the previous Exercises, you are now able to plan and write a complete essay without being told step by step what to do. You have absorbed the steps and can now go through the process almost automatically. Prove that you can do it on your own by planning and writing an essay of at least 500 words. Draw up an outline, write the essay, and then proofread it carefully before you recopy and turn it in to your instructor. Choose from the following topics or a similar one assigned or approved by your instructor:

a) How Can One Cope with Loneliness?
b) Mistakes Parents Make
c) America's Greatest Problem
d) Adjusting to Aging Parents
e) Is Censorship Justified?
f) Should Eighteen-Year-Olds Vote?
g) What Education Should Be
h) Religious Themes in Contemporary Literature

Answer Key

This answer key has been included to let you check your answers quickly and conveniently. Please do not use it until you have finished working an exercise completely. Otherwise, you will gain nothing from this workbook. Your instructor will not be grading the exercises (except for an occasional complete paragraph or essay). Therefore, looking ahead at the answers will gain you nothing and lose you much. Also, any time your answer differs from the one given here, check carefully to determine why you missed that question. You may sometimes find that you have given a slightly different answer from the one here. Don't panic. Simply try to understand why yours differs. In a few instances, there is more than one possible answer to a question and this will usually be indicated in the key. However, if it is not, and you feel your answer may be equally correct, check with your instructor to make sure.

STEP 1 •

1.	G	S	5.	G	S	9.	G	S	13.	G	S
2.	G	S	6.	S	G	10.	S	G	14.	G	S
3.	S	G	7.	G	S	11.	G	S	15.	G	S
4.	G	S	8.	G	S	12.	G	S	16.	G	S
									17.	S	G

STEP 2 •

1.	1	6	5	3	2	4	5.	1	4	2	5	3
2.	5	3	1	2	4		6.	5	2	4	3	1
3.	1	4	3	2	5		7.	2	4	3	1	5
4.	4	5	1	2	3		8.	4	2	5	3	1

STEP 3 • EXERCISE A •

1.	f	3.	b	5.	d	7.	e	9.	b	11.	b	13.	b
2.	d	4.	c	6.	a	8.	d	10.	d	12.	d		

STEP 3 • EXERCISE B •

Answers will vary
1. transportation
2. pets (or animals)
3. languages (or nationalities)
4. making a decision
5. preparing to study (or preparing to write a term paper)
6. studying a poem
7. Typing has many advantages for the student
8. My driving instructor is scared to death.
9. The sons of famous men are rarely as renowned as their fathers.
10. Chad is an expert at procrastinating before writing a paper.

STEP 4 •

The ordering of specifics can vary as long as you have the right numbers on each chart. However, the number you place beside the *GS* must correspond to what is given here.

1. SP b	SP c	3. SP a	SP b
SP e	SP d	SP c	SP d
SP f	SP h	SP g	SP f
SP g	SP cars	SP h	SP visiting Washington
GS cars	GS a	GS visiting Washington	GS e

2. SP a	SP b	4. SP a	SP c
SP d	SP e	SP b	SP e
SP f	SP g	SP d	SP f
SP h	SP flower	SP g	SP The invention. . .
GS flower	GS c	GS The invention. . .	GS h

STEP 5 •

Answers will vary. Check to be sure your answers are of the same *type* as those given here. Are all your specifics "contained" in the general item?

1. dolls, games, electric trains, blocks
2. baseball, basketball, football, soccer
3. gathering equipment, soaping the car, scrubbing the wheels, rinsing the car off thoroughly
4. stocking up on suntan lotion, packing a lunch, filling an ice chest with plenty of cold drinks, loading the car
5. scanning the headlines, checking scores on the sports page, chuckling over the comics, disagreeing with the editorial page thoughtfully
6. We travel more than our parents did. Young people can get away from home easily. We choke on smog created by auto exhaust. A shopping trip downtown is easy and convenient.
7. They treat their students fairly. They show interest in each member of the class. They are intelligent, well-informed, and articulate. They see their students as people, not things.

STEP 6 •

1. Even in the midst of crowds of people, many are lonely.
2. Our trip to Washington, D.C. was the high point of the summer.
3. Young people derive their morals from many sources.
4. A well-planned mass transit network offers many advantages to a city and its citizens.
5. An alligator must have a natural-like environment in order to survive in captivity.
6. The instincts of animals seem to enable them to preserve their health more efficiently than does the vaunted intelligence of human beings.
7. In short, though one cannot know what death is like, having never experienced it, some situations which arise in daily life seem as if they must surely be worse than dying.

STEP 7 •

Answers will vary. Check to make sure your answers are of the same *type* as those given here. Is your topic sentence general enough to summarize all the specifics? Is it a complete sentence?

1. A lush, green lawn does not happen by accident.
2. Reading a textbook assignment effectively requires careful work.
3. Photography is an interesting and profitable hobby.
4. Hunting is a necessary part of good wildlife conservation.

STEP 8 •

1. b f   2. d f   3. c f   4. b d g   5. b f   6. c e g   7. d f

STEP 9 •

Answers will vary. Check to be sure your answers are similar in form to those suggested here. Are your specifics all "contained" in the general statement given?

1. Drivers with CB's are more friendly than in the past.
   They are more likely to stop to help another motorist.
   They are less suspicious of other motorists.
   They tend to be more cooperative and less competitive.
2. They establish limits that are reasonable.
   They are willing to listen to the child's point of view.
   They change rules that turn out to be unfair.
   They do not hesitate to admit that they were wrong.
3. Possessing a driver's license is only the beginning; skillful driving requires years of practice.
   Tips from experienced drivers can be helpful.
   Thoughtful evaluation of one's own weaknesses leads to improvement.
   Serious commitment to becoming a good driver is required.
4. The mood swings of the young person can be bewildering.
   Suddenly, the young person becomes very secretive about his or her activities.

The parents are constantly the target for irrational anger.
It is painful to see one's "baby" growing more independent.

STEP 10 •

Did you use the general statement given as the first sentence of your paragraph?
Did you indent the first line? Did you explain each specific in an additional
sentence or two?

STEP 11 •

Is your general statement a complete sentence? Are all your specifics "contained"
in the general statement?

STEP 12 •

Did you indent the first line and keep the margins straight? Did you clarify each
specific with extra explanatory information? Did you underline the topic
sentence and number the specifics, as shown in the example?

STEP 13 • EXERCISE A •

1. GS: It is relatively easy to improve the coherence of one's writing. (Second
sentence might also be considered the topic sentence.)
   SP: The use of logical connectors, for example, or transitional devices
   as they are sometimes called, is an aid to clear, logical writing.
       EX: Readers need all the help they can get, and a well-placed
       however, for example, or *therefore* can add immeasurably to
       ease of reading.
   SP: The use of pronouns is another simple means of improving coherence.
       EX: Every pronoun correctly used refers to an antecedent in the
       same or preceding sentence and serves, in effect, to weave the
       writing together, as in a mesh.
   SP: A third way even a novice writer can make writing flow logically
   and fluently is to develop the habit of consistency.
       EX: The writer who begins a paragraph writing about *people*
       should stick with *people,* and not switch to *a person* or *you* or
       we; and a narrative begun in the past tense should not switch
       to the present tense or to the future conditional for no
       apparent reason.
   SP: Even more important, however, than all of these means of achieving coherence in writing is the habit of filling in all the gaps in
   thinking.
       EX: The writer who depends on the reader's willingness to infer
       what is not said is asking a great deal, and even a skillful and
       interested reader is likely to feel that the author has not
       provided a complete and lucid piece of writing.
2. GS: The club consisted of four distinct groups of personalities.
   SP: Most vocal were those members who were totally devoted to the
   president and supported her in everything she suggested.

EX: The president had only to make her wishes known and these obedient followers immediately wheeled into line behind her, marshalling arguments and hustling votes.

EX: One got the impression that they would vote for their own execution if the president called for it.

SP: These members were opposed, of course, by an equally vigorous group which automatically disapproved of any plan that emanated from the president's camp.

EX: They would have vetoed their own elevation to the peerage if their nomination had come from the president or one of her supporters.

SP: A third group of members, less serious in intent, enjoyed themselves by stirring up trouble, asking questions with embarrassing answers and bringing up subjects the more earnest members would rather have left buried.

EX: They had no real interest in how issues were settled or which faction controlled the group; they simply enjoyed thrusting themselves forward in ways that discomfited the leaders.

SP: Their antics saved the day for the fourth group, comprised of inert individuals who were not even interested enough to cause trouble, but who sometimes roused themselves enough to cast the deciding vote for the group whose performance pleased them most.

EX: They were a group to be reckoned with, a group whose power to determine the future of the club far exceeded any contribution they made to it.

STEP 13 • EXERCISE B •

Answers will vary. Check your paragraphs against the examples below, which contain adequate extending information.

1. While television shows are reasonably good, the commercials that accompany them are a disgrace. One of the many bad features of commercials is their loudness. They seem to be twice as loud as the program and the viewer is almost deafened when they come on. Any attempt at conversation during commercials is futile. Commercials also take up too much time and are repeated too often. The impression one usually gets is that the shows are sandwiched in between long periods of advertising, all of it the same. Often commercials interrupt a show at a particularly inappropriate time. Just when the program is getting exciting, just as the plot begins to thicken, or the long-awaited star is about to come on, the announcer reports that, "we will be back after this message." Too many commercials insult the viewers' intelligence by presenting unrealistic situations and senseless dialogue. Tornadoes and doves rip in and out of kitchens, white knights gallop through backyards, and employees declare to their bosses that they have bad breath. It seems that, rather than inducing the

viewers to buy a product, commercials are deliberately planned to turn them against it.

2. Every season of the year brings its gift of beauty to the lover of nature. Spring offers welcome delights that make it the favorite season of many. Fruit trees burst into flower, soft clouds driven by playful winds scamper across the sky, and birds noisily go about the task of setting up housekeeping. Summer offers a very different kind of beauty, more lively, bright and vigorous. Pastel spring flowers give way to the vivid hues of sturdy annuals, and budding trees turn lush with deep green foliage. Autumn's beauty has a dual nature, expressing the ripeness of harvest along with the sense of ending, of closing down for winter, that follows. Bright leaves drop to the ground forming a crunchy carpet that soon turns dusty brown. Even winter, for all its absence of vividness and growth, has colors of its own that give particular pleasure to the sensitive beholder. The stark black outline of a tree against a dull grey sky or caps of snow piled high on chubby evergreens are no less thrilling than what has come before or what will return with spring.

STEP 14 •

Is your general statement a complete sentence? Are all your specifics related to the general statement? Did you underline the topic sentence, number the specifics, and label the extenders?

STEP 15 • EXERCISE A •

1. *Topic Sentence:* The owner of a pet alligator should protect it by placing it in a pen of some sort.
   Clincher: All of these dangers can be eliminated if the owner keeps the pet in a fenced off pond or in a pen.
2. *Topic sentence:* A snowfall in late spring brings a special excitement as two seasons manifest themselves at once.
   No Clincher
3. *Topic sentence:* A home decorating precept worth considering is that every room should contain something alive.
   No Clincher
4. *Topic sentence:* If you are to learn to study efficiently, you must become a good notetaker.
   No Clincher
5. *Topic sentence:* Everywhere they turn today Americans are confronted with the message that they can stay youthful forever.
   No Clincher
6. *Topic sentence:* Joan's greatest disappointment was the time she went to a dude ranch in Utah for her vacation.

Clincher: She was grateful for such pleasures; however, that vacation remained in her memory as a dismal and disappointing experience.

7. *Topic sentence:* This truly spectacular tourist attraction is well worth a special trip to St. Louis.

8. *Topic sentence:* The starting time of a sports event is often delayed or changed because of television.
   No Clincher

9. *Topic sentence:* Every high school student, therefore, should learn to type because of the many advantages which typing has over script. (The first sentence in this paragraph presents specifics and is not a topic sentence.)

STEP 15 • EXERCISE B •

Did you place the general statement (topic sentence) at the end of your paragraph? Is it a complete sentence? Is it general enough to include all the specifics? Are all your specifics directly related to this statement? Did you remember to underline the topic sentence, number the specifics, and label the extenders?

STEP 15 • EXERCISE C •

Did you place the general statement (topic sentence) at the beginning of the paragraph? Is it a complete sentence? Does it include all the specifics contained in the paragraph? Are all your specifics directly related to the general statement? Did you write a clincher sentence at the end? Does it restate the topic sentence in *different words*? Did you underline both the topic sentence and clincher, number the specifics and label the extenders?

STEP 16 • EXERCISE A •

Note that some of the specifics fall into more than one category.

1. a. fact or reason
   b. reason
   c. incident
   d. fact or reason
   e. reason
   f. fact

2. a. fact
   b. example or incident
   c. fact
   d. example
   e. fact

3. a. reason
   b. fact or example
   c. example
   d. example or incident
   e. example

STEP 16 • EXERCISE B •

1. examples or facts
2. reasons
3. facts
4. facts
5. incident
6. reasons or examples
7. incident
8. reasons or examples
9. incident
10. facts

STEP 16 • EXERCISE C •

Is your general statement a complete sentence. Did you use *facts* as the specifics in your paragraph? Are all your facts related directly to the general statement?

Did you provide adequate extending explanation between your specifics? Did you underline the topic sentence, number the specifics, and label the extenders?

STEP 16 • EXERCISE D •

Is your general statement a complete sentence? Did you use *examples* as the specifics in your paragraph? Are all your examples directly related to the general statement? Did you provide adequate extending explanation between your specifics? Did you underline the topic sentence, number the specifics, and label the extenders?

STEP 16 • EXERCISE E •

Is your topic sentence a general statement of the main idea of the paragraph and not part of the incident you use to explain it? Is your supporting incident explained in detail? Have you used only *one* incident? Did you underline the topic sentence and clincher, number the specifics, and label the extenders?

STEP 16 • EXERCISE F •

Is your general statement a complete sentence? Have you underlined it? Do all of your specifics answer the question "why"? Did you provide adequate connecting detail between your reasons? Did you underline the topic sentence, number the specifics, and label the extenders?

STEP 17 •

1. examples, incident, reasons
2. examples, incident, reasons
3. examples, incident, reasons
4. examples, incident, reasons
5. facts
6. examples, incident, facts
7. examples, incident, reasons
8. examples, reasons
9. incident, facts
10. examples, reasons
11. reasons, facts
12. examples, incident, reasons

STEP 18 • EXERCISE A •

1. comparison/contrast, type b
2. time
3. comparison/contrast, type a
4. importance
5. comparison/contrast, type b
6. time
7. importance

STEP 18 • EXERCISE B •

1. time (2 4 1 3)
2. comparison/contrast: either
   type a (1 3 4 2 5 6) or
   type b (1 6 3 5 4 2)
3. position (2 4 6 1 3 5)
4. time or difficulty (2 4 3 1)
5. time (6 3 1 5 2 4)
6. problem to answer (3 5 1 4 2)

STEP 18 • EXERCISE C •

Have you used a different order of specifics in each of your three paragraphs?
Did you write in the appropriate blanks the *order* to be used? Are all of your
general statements complete sentences? Did you underline topic sentences and
clinchers and number specifics? Did you explain each specific adequately and
provide extending information? *Save these paragraphs. You'll need them in
Step 19.*

STEP 19 • EXERCISE A •

1. a) In addition (listing)   b) Furthermore (listing)   c Besides (listing)
   d) Finally (listing)   e) Therefore (results)
2. a) at one moment (time)   b) for example (example)   c) but (contrast)
   d) furthermore (listing)   e) and (listing)   f) but (contrast)
3. a) for one thing (listing)   b) also (listing)   c) for instance (example)
   d) hence (result)   e) in addition (listing)   f) therefore
   g) also (listing)
4. a) For instance (example)   b) however (contrast)   f) nor (listing)
   d) whereas (contrast)   e) on the contrary (contrast)   f) nor (listing)
5. a) thus (result)   b) for instance (example)   c) true (emphasis)
   d) indeed (emphasis)   e) nor listing   f) after all (emphasis)
   g) in fact (emphasis)   h) as a matter of fact (emphasis)
6. a) but even more (contrast)   b) first (listing)   c) second (listing)
   d) as a matter of fact (emphasis)   e) then (results)   f) or (listing)

STEP 19 • EXERCISE C •

Did you indicate what order you were going to use? Did you supply the needed
signal words?

STEP 20 • EXERCISE A •

1. b (for instance)
2. b (he . . . it)
3. a (But . . . those)
4. b (Consequently)
5. a (Others . . . however)
6. a (Ever since that time)
7. b (Another)

8. a (One fruit . . .)
9. a (It)
10. a (But they . . . this)

STEP 20 • EXERCISE B •

1. He practiced law in my home town for thirty-five years.
2. Then (or Next), find the dog and lure him into the tub.
3. For example, he turns the novel into a play at several points.
4. This action had an effect on most of the countries in the Western World.
5. One advantage is that (or For example,) most of one's education can be planned with the chosen career in mind.
6. One of the things that made him a great president was that (or For example,) he inspired the youth of this country.
7. This brave man (or For example, he) had to place himself in a machine that could become a coffin traveling at 600 miles per hour at any moment.
8. But (or However or On the other hand), at the Chinese Castle they are asked not to smoke at all.
9. In addition (or Also), she sings very well.
10. Therefore (or As a result), he was not qualified for the position he held.
11. Then you are ready to begin writing.

STEP 20 • EXERCISE C •

Check your paragraph to make sure that the relationships among the ideas are made perfectly clear and that it flows smoothly from one idea to the next.

STEP 21 • EXERCISE B •

1. A professional athlete sometimes becomes the public's darling for a season or more for reasons not easy to fathom. The athlete may wear his hair a way that catches the fancy of the fans, or he may become dear to the fans because of unusually romantic or poignant circumstances of a personal nature.

2. Baseball players are accustomed to hazards that cause a number of injuries each season. They are used to having to slide into a pair of waiting spikes. They face pitches which come in at a speed of up to 90 miles an hour, and boldly face up to pitchers who have a reputation for being willing to dust back a threatening batter.

3. Oranges are an important part of a complete diet. They have much more vitamin C than apples, which are considered so very nutritious. Similarly, oranges are as good a source of potassium as bananas, which are recommended as a source of that mineral.

STEP 22 • EXERCISE B •

1. The patient and watchful mother gives finger food to the baby, who promptly pitches it to the floor. Mother picks it up. Again she gives food to the baby, and

again he pitches it to the floor. The game continues, with the mother giving food to the baby and the baby gleefully tossing it on the floor. It is not easy to predict whether the mother or the baby will win the playful tug of war.

2. First, the librarians spread out on tables the new material they wished to catalogue and shelve. They noted all the necessary information and integrated it into existing records, preparatory to offering the new material to the public. They accomplished the task in far less time than they had anticipated.

3. The parents decided that the children could make the garden that year. They went with the children to the garden shop and advised them what seeds to buy, and when the ground was ready, told them it was time to begin. The children carried everything—seeds, tools, watering cans and hoses—to the garden plot and began their hard work. They had all the vegetables planted in no time at all and marked each row to show what seeds they had planted there.

STEP 23 •

1. Many young women are planning careers which they hope will make them financially independent. They are no longer satisfied to be wholly dependent on their husbands. They wish to make their own mark in the world while, at the same time, making a marriage which will be emotionally fulfilling. They seem confident that they can handle these dual roles with ease. Many of them would like to have children, but they realize there are other options. They no longer see child bearing as their obligatory function. They seem unaware that their plans might be somewhat threatening to the kind of young man they hope to marry. They do not seem to know that some young men are fearful of liberated women and hope to marry a girl who will be content to look up to them and be happy caring for their meals, laundry and children.

2. The picnic was to be on Monday. That was the only really convenient day that week. As luck would have it, it rained on Monday, and the group had to choose another day. Tuesday was out of the question because so many of the members had a meeting to attend that day. Wednesday was not much better, because so many people had to work that night and would have to leave early. But the picnic was finally set for Wednesday afternoon, and in spite of all the shifts in plans, everyone had a good time.

3. There were 203 people in the graduating class. For one reason or another, however, only 198 were present for commencement. As a result, there were five empty seats in the front row, which raised questions in the minds of the spectators. People tried to determine who was absent by checking the alphabetical list on the program. This was not very helpful, however, since the young people were hard to identify with their caps and gowns on. As curious as they were, the spectators had to wait and see which students did not appear to receive a diploma when their names were called. Then the mystery was solved.

4. Teenage marriages face many obstacles. Among them are the problems which arise when an inexperienced and undereducated young man faces the need to make a living. It is almost impossible for a young fellow who has not finished his schooling to make an adequate income to support a wife and, perhaps, a child in a pleasant home environment. As a consequence, many young married couples are forced to live with one set of parents or the other while the young man continues his schooling. Young people, unfortunately, are seldom prepared to recognize and cope with the problems of homemaking. They are not accus-

tomed to coping with bills that come in regularly every month for rent, food, clothes and transportation. Learning to cope with these obligations is a very sobering experience. As time passes, of course, the young couple will continue to mature and grow in their capacity to cope with an adult pattern of life. Unfortunately, however, they may grow into very different, even incompatible, people. He may become a very serious minded young businessman, and she may grow into a young woman eager to go out, herself, into the business world, rather than to stay home to be a sheltered wife and mother.

STEP 24 •

Answers will vary. Compare your revision to the example given in the explanation preceding the exercise. Is yours as effective? Have you followed all four of the guidelines?

STEP 25 •

One who wishes to do some writing should first of all find a quiet, well-lighted place with no distracting noises. The place one chooses should have a level surface large enough for all the books, papers, and materials that one needs. All these materials should be gathered before beginning to write, since it is a waste of time to constantly have to stop and go running after a dictionary or thesaurus. The time one chooses to write is also important. Generally it should be at a time convenient to the author, but it should not begin too late in the evening. Breaks in writing time are very necessary, since one cannot be expected to concentrate for long periods without a rest. In fact, research studies show that writers are more efficient if they write about forty-five minutes and take a ten-minute break. One should be careful, though, that the "break" time does not exceed the amount of time actually spent writing. Once the writer has found the proper environment for work and has established a time to begin, the real work starts. Writing is a complex process that requires concentration. If one has background material to read, the reading should be done actively, with an attempt to remember the points one plans to cover in the writing. (The next sentence in the original is an unrelated specific; eliminate it.) If one has taken notes which need to be reviewed, one should do more than skim over them half-heartedly. The practised writer will be thinking of possible situations to develop from these notes. By doing this, one can make full use of the material. Writers who take care to follow these steps when they write will find that the effort pays off in more and better writing for less effort.

STEP 27 • EXERCISE A •

JOINING THE PEACE CORPS

Introduction { The American Peace Corps, established during the administration of President John F. Kennedy, has proven once and for all that Americans will literally go to the ends of the earth to work for a better, more peaceful world. For little monetary return, but for the satisfaction of significant work and foreign

{ travel, hundreds of thousands of American citizens have applied for an opportunity to serve abroad in the Peace Corps. Unfortunately, many applicants have had to be turned away. A great deal more than willing hands and an eager heart is required to perform successfully in the Corps. In order to be sure that the most qualified applicants are accepted, a complex procedure governing application has been set up. The applicant must meet certain qualifications, respond to questionnaires and examinations, and go through a period of training.

Applicants must have certain qualifications. [1] First, they must be at least eighteen years old and citizens of the United States. [2] They can be married, but if a couple wants to serve, both partners must have suitable skills. [3] A third qualification is vocational skill. This term means that applicants must already know how to do something, such as teaching or farming, because the program has no provision for training people in the skills that will later be imparted to others. Neither a college education nor prior knowledge of a foreign language is required, however. [4] Another qualification is that applicants must not have any serious physical, mental or emotional disturbance. [5] Most important of all, though, they must be willing to work hard for two years.

If their qualifications meet Peace Corps standards, applicants must provide various kinds of information. [1] First, they must fill out a questionnaire, listing skills, hobbies, educational level achieved, schools attended, special interests, and work background, if any. [2] Applicants must also provide references from friends, teachers, and/or employers. [3] Furthermore, they must take placement tests—which are noncompetitive and test aptitudes and ability to learn foreign languages. A volunteer is picked for training on the basis of the information given on the questionnaire, the aptitude and ability shown on the tests, and references submitted.

After taking the tests, chosen volunteers must go through a training period of approximately twelve weeks at a United States training center or in the assigned country. [1] During this time volunteers are taught a great deal about the country in which they will be working. They study its history and culture. [2] They are also given technical, physical, and health training to enable them to remain healthy while living under conditions that are not always the most healthful. [3] Another important part of the training is learning the language of the assigned country. A volunteer can expect at least 300 hours of language instruction. When the period of training ends, final selections of volunters are made.

After the final selections, successful volunteers are sent to a foreign country for two years of service. By the time these two years are completed, they understand that the initial selection and training process was worthwhile.

STEP 27 • EXERCISE B •

Today's teenagers encounter many problems in their diversified lives Nevertheless, few teenagers ever discuss their worries with their parents—the two people who love them most and want the best for them—but prefer to talk about the problems with friends. Most adults feel they are aware of their teenager's problems and are readily available to help solve them. But teenagers often fail to bring their problems before their parents because they sense in them distrust, preoccupation, and a lack of understanding—all of which seem to be contributing factors in this unfortunate failure to communicate.

Many adolescents feel that an older person, such as a parent, is unable to relate to the problems of the present day youth. Some parents fail to understand because of the [1] different environment in which they grew up, which produced different experiences and problems. For example, most parents see "going steady" as undesirable, even though most teenagers do it. The reason they dislike this practice is that when they were young it meant the couple was planning to be engaged soon. Now, of course, this is not the case. Other parents tend to [2] underestimate the pressures on today's students, such as the necessity of getting superior grades in high school. When they were ready to go to college, the main requirement was having enough money. Today, however, it is necessary for students to be in the upper fifth of their class to be admitted to a competitive university. Such things may be extremely important to the teen, yet can seem merely foolish to an adult who does not realize the seriousness of the problem. [3] Parents also fail to realize the change in life style their teenagers are making. They often cannot accept the fact that the dependent adolescent is changing into a self-reliant adult. Along with this change emerge added responsibilities and privileges. When giving advice, however, many parents act as though they were addressing a young child rather than someone who is almost an adult. Because of this lack of understanding on the parents' part, teenagers feel they have no choice but to turn to their friends, who have similar problems and are more apt to be more understanding. Simple misunderstandings then, such as those mentioned here, may become major stumbling blocks to attempts at communication between teenager and parent.

Distrust is another cause for this lack of communication. While parents may say they trust their teenagers, their actions often indicate otherwise. For example, [1] many parents listen in on their children's phone calls or open their mail, because they do not trust them to behave themselves properly. Also, [2] parents frequently impose unreasonable restrictions on the activities of their teenaged children, simply because they do not trust their judgement. No young person is going to talk openly to an adult who shows no faith in the teen's intelligence or actions. Furthermore, [3] many parents demonstrate quite clearly that they are not deserving of trust themselves. It may be that they simply repeat to another person in the family something told to them in confidence, but to many teens this is an act of disloyalty. When this kind of mutual distrust develops, the lines of communication break down.

Another reason teenagers do not bring their problems to their parents is that the parents are often too busy or too wrapped up in their own lives to give them the attention they need. To some parents, [1] social commitments are more important than being at home to discuss the problems of their children. Or [2] they feel that they can fulfill their responsibilities by giving their children money and a car. Some father, for example, are so busy working to provide these material comforts for their families that they have no time left to spend with their children. [3] Even the television set can become an obstacle between parents and children. It is next to impossible for teenagers to bring their problems before their parents when they are sitting glued to the screen all evening, every evening. Parents who are too involved with their own activities to notice their teenagers' problems force them to seek advice elsewhere. (In such families,) lack of communication is due to the parents' selfishness.

Lack of communication between the generations will continue until adults realize that teenagers are maturing individuals who need attention, understanding, and respectful trust. Lack of any of (these) elements in the parents' attitude will always create barriers between teenager and parent. (These) carriers must be broken and conquered before meaningful communication can begin.

STEP 27 • EXERCISE C •

Thesis Sentence: But teenagers often fail to bring their problems before their parents because they sense in them distrust, preoccupation, and a lack of understanding—all of which seem to be contributing factors in this unfortunate failure to communicate.

First Main Point: parents' lack of understanding
> GS (*Topic Sentence*) Many adolescents feel that an older person, such as a parent, is unable to relate to the problems of the present day youth.
> SP different environment in which parents grew up
> SP underestimation of the pressures on today's students
> SP failure to realize the change of life style their children are making

Second Main Point: mutual distrust
> GS (*Topic Sentence*) Distrust is another cause for this lack of communication.
> SP actions that demonstrate parents' lack of trust in their children
> SP imposition of unreasonable restrictions on teens
> SP untrustworthy actions of parents themselves

Third Main Point: parents' preoccupation with their own activities
> GS (*Topic Sentence*) Another reason teenagers do not bring their problems to their parents is that the parents are often too busy or too wrapped up in their own lives to give them the attention they need.
> SP greater interest in their own social commitments than in their children's problems
> SP attempts to fulfill their family obligations with material gifts
> SP the interference of television

STEP 28 • EXERCISE A •

1. dogs
2. job security
3. peace
4. sugar
5. industry or greed

6. youth
7. beauty
8. money
9. writing
10. old age

STEP 28 • EXERCISE B •

Answers will, of course, vary. Following are some possibilities:

1. Public education in many areas needs sources of funding other than the tax on property.
2. Public schools as the purveyors of attitudes and values face strong competition from commercial television.
3. Students in their teens often do not consider it important to learn what middle-aged teachers think is important to teach.
4. Access to exercise facilities is becoming a popular fringe benefit offered to employees of large corporations.
5. Prenatal care determines the health of a baby to a significant extent.
6. The capacity to be alone without being lonely is one that comes with the growth of self-awareness.
7. Much crime is committed by single young men who do not belong to a family that cares about them.
8. The beauty of autumn is made more poignant by the fact that it will so soon be gone.
9. In commercial terms, a piece of artwork is worth whatever it can bring in the marketplace.
10. One who has known much sorrow will more deeply appreciate joy.

STEP 28 • EXERCISE C •

Answers will, of course, vary. Following are some possibilities:

1. Loneliness — Lonely people are vulnerable to the appeal of cults.
2. Good Health — Some daily exercise is essential to good health at any age.
3. Guilt — Expressions of anger are often an unconscious means of disguising feelings of guilt.
4. Deception — No friendship can thrive in the presence of deliberate deception.

STEP 29 • EXERCISE A •

1. b   Other choice is merely a statement of fact, shows no opinion.
2. b   Other choice is not a complete sentence.
3. b   Other choice is merely a statement of fact, shows no opinion.
4. a   Other choice is not a complete sentence.
5. a   Other choice indicates no opinion.
6. a   Other choice is not a complete sentence.
7. b   Other choice is merely a statement of fact, shows no opinion.
8. b   Other choice merely expresses a personal preference.
9. a   Other choice is not as precise and qualified.
10. b   Other choice is not as precise and qualified.
11. b   Other choice is simply an expression of personal preference.

12. b   Other choice is too general, not adequately limited.
13. b   Other choice is too general and vague.
14. b   Other choice is too general and vague.
15. b   Other choice is too general and vague.
16. b   Other choice is not a complete sentence.
17. a   Other choice is imprecise.
18. b   Other choice is merely a statement of fact or personal preference.
19. b   Other choice is a statement of fact, shows no opinion.
20. a   Other choice is a statement of fact, shows no opinion.
21. b   Other choice is general and imprecise.
22. b   Other choice is merely a statement of fact, shows no opinion.
23. b   Other choiuce is not a complete sentence.
24 a   Other choice is not a complete sentence.
25. b   Other choice is a statement of fact, shows no opinion.
26. b   Other choice does not show an opinion.

STEP 30 •

1. E
2. C
3. A
4. D
5. B
6. A
7. A
8. E
9. B
10. D
11. C

STEP 31 •

Does your thesis sentence meet the requirements listed in Step 29? Did you indicate the order of specifics you plan to use by writing it in the appropriate blank for each paragraph? Did you add the necessary signal words to your outline?

STEP 32 •

Does your thesis sentence appear in the introductory paragraph? Did you use at least one complete paragraph for each of your main points? Did you write a good concluding paragraph? Did you place a wavy line under the thesis, underline topic sentences, number specifics, and circle signal words?

STEP 33 • EXERCISE A •

Does your *funnel* introduction begin with an idea that is more general than any other in the paragraph, including your thesis? Is the last idea in your paragraph the thesis? Is it the most specific idea in the introduction? Have you provided the steps in between—gradually becoming more and more specific as you move toward the thesis? Do your ideas flow smoothly from one to another? (If you detect problems with smoothness, you may need to review Steps 19–23.)

STEP 33 • EXERCISE B •

Does your *contrast* introduction fall into two parts—the first presenting a commonly held belief, and the second presenting a thesis which contradicts or modifies this belief? Did you use some sort of signal word to indicate the contradiction? Did you explain in several sentences the commonly held belief that begins your paragraph?

STEP 33 • EXERCISE C •

Does your *anecdotal* introduction begin with a brief story or incident? Does it end with the thesis sentence? Is your anecdote interesting enough to capture the interest of the reader? Have you limited yourself to one incident, saving others for use later in the essay as illustrations?

STEP 33 • EXERCISE D •

1. Thesis: Next to last sentence
   Type: Contrast
   Factors: generosity of spirit, respect for self, respect for others
2. Thesis: Last sentence
   Type: Funnel
   Factors: openness, honesty and concern, progress without defense of status quo
3. Thesis: Last sentence
   Type: Anecdotal
   Factors: be a good listener, be receptive to strangers and lonely people, be appreciative of others' efforts
4. Thesis: Last sentence
   Type: Contrast
   Factors: No preview
5. Thesis: Last sentence
   Type: Funnel
   Factors: No preview
6. Thesis Last sentence
   Type: Anecdotal
   Factors: No preview
7. Thesis: Last sentence
   Factors: sports foster physical fitness, make young people more responsible, sports help young people function better in a group

STEP 34 • EXERCISE A •

1. b also
2. b Another
3. a At the same time
4. a Despite the obvious importance of the past, however
5. b As a result of this trusting atmosphere in the group
6. a these
7. a They, however, such
8. b Nevertheless
9. a Likewise

10. b First
11. b Having shown that French resistance forces led all others in providing help to the Allied armies
12. a The Spurts were by no means the only club whose strategies . . .

STEP 35 •

Were you careful to avoid repeating your ideas in exactly the same words as they were expressed earlier in the essay? Which of the suggestions did you attempt to incorporate into your conclusion?

STEP 36 • EXERCISE B •

A person who wakes up in the night and smells smoke should immediately rouse other family members and get them out of the house. If, however, access to other parts of the house is cut off, the person should not delay, but should immediately get himself or herself out of the building and try to reach other family members through other doors and windows.

STEP 36 • EXERCISE C •

Persons who wake up in the night and smell smoke should immediately rouse other family members and get them out of the house. If, however, their access to other parts of the house is cut off, they should not delay, but should immediately get themselves out of the building and try to reach their family through other doors and windows.

STEP 36 • EXERCISE I •

Answers will vary, of course. The following is one possibility.

1. The first candidate to be considered is one whose face is well known to anyone who has been active in city politics during the last ten years. With his fine mind and high moral character he would undoubtedly make an important contribution to the work of the council.

2. The second candidate to be considered is an exceptional person, Mrs. Norma Brown. She has been praised by all who know her many achievements both as a lawyer and as a worker for charitable causes. She possesses a rare combination of love for hard work and unshakable good nature.

STEP 36 • EXERCISE K •

Answers will vary, of course. The following is one possibility.

It is a privilege to know Mrs. Brown personally. Her grace of manner is such that her campaign workers revere her as if she were a much older woman. Her youth, however, belies her years of faithful and much praised service in the mayor's office, where those who know her agree that she has accepted the praise accorded her with rare and becoming modesty.

STEP 36 • EXERCISE M •

Answers will vary, of course. The following is one possibility.

The group usually was able to interact in a way that was satisfactory to most members. When the discussion became intense, however, some of the quieter members felt as if the more vocal members dominated the discussion and made it impossible for them to get a fair share of attention. As a consequence, the group found it necessary occasionally to cease discussing the subject with which it was concerned at the moment and, instead, talk about their own problems of communication, making sure that all members had an opportunity to express their feelings. The moderator did her best to keep the group interacting in an open and trusting way, but she, after all, was only one person and a rather unassertive one at that, and it was the members themselves who, as they worked out their problems together, managed to forge a close-knit group that was able to accomplish a great deal.

STEP 36 • EXERCISE N •

Answers will vary, of course. The following is offered as one possibility.

When he finally laid down his work to rest his mind for a moment, he walked over and looked out the window. He was surprised to notice two men cursing loudly at one another in a very vulgar manner. Shortly, before he could gain any understanding of what was going on, a police officer came running down the street shouting loudly at the two men and waving his stick threateningly. It was immediately evident that the two men had no desire to meet the officer, and they raced off in opposite directions leaving him scratching his head and wondering what had been the trouble between the two men.

STEP 37 • EXERCISE A •

There are over a quarter million automobiles sold in the United States each year. Many types are available—foreign cars and American cars, convertibles and sedans, big cars and little cars. This variety is the result of the wide range of tastes of the driving population. Of these, there are three kinds of cars which do not suit my taste at all and which I would never own. One type is impractical, another is little and ugly, and a third is poorly made.

An example of an impractical car is the Excalibur SS. Most people have never seen one of these cars. It bears a strong resemblance to the Dusenberg of years ago or to an old MG, early 1951 or 1952. One of the things I do not like about it is that it only comes in a convertible model. That is fine in the summer or on a sunny day, but when it rains or when winter comes, it is rather impractical. Winter is perhaps the roughest, though, mainly because the car is not even equipped with a heater. And the softtop has plastic side windows and a plastic rear window that leak and yellow in the sun and become brittle with age. This car is fitted with a 327 cubic inch engine from the Corvette Stingray. But it does not weigh more than 2000 pounds, compared to the Corvette, which weighs approximately 3200 pounds this year. With over 350 horsepower and so little weight, the Excalibur is very dangerous. One cannot come near controlling it on acceleration around curves or on a panic stop. Combining these shortcomings with a $10,000 price tag, one has a very impractical car.

Another car that I would not want is one of these ugly little foreign "bugs" one sees everywhere. The Volkswagen is a good example. This simply is not my idea of an attractive car. In addition, it is too small for safety. If one were hit in the side by a large car or by a truck, one would probably not survive. One also cannot ride for great distances in comfort, because the engine is too noisy and the interior is cramped. Another shortcoming is that Volkswagens are too common. I do not want a car that everyone else has, and if one looks around any large parking lot in this city, one is sure to see at least ten Volkswagens. Besides being so common, this car is too underpowered for freeway driving. It is almost impossible to pass a car on the expressway at fifty-five miles per hour, and if there is a stiff crosswind blowing, the driver would think he or she was on a roller coaster. This is both unpleasant and unsafe.

The third type of car that I would not like to own is one that is cheaply made. Ford Mustangs fall into this class. My family owned one once, and before we sold it the muffler fell off at least five times. By then there were rattles in every corner. Meanwhile, the paint had started peeling off, to say nothing of the first layer of chrome on the bumpers. Furthermore, whenever the driver made a hard left turn, the door on the passenger's side would fly open. (*The last sentence in the original version is an unrelated specific; eliminate it.*)

Although I consider myself to be a fairly reasonable person, who can understand that different people like different kinds of cars, I simply cannot understand why anybody would buy the cars I have described here. If they are impractical, I do not want them. If they are "buggy," forget it. And if they are cheap, please leave them on the display floor, because I am not interested.

If you did not spot all of these errors when proofreading, you may have weakness in grammar, punctuation, or spelling. See your instructor for additional help.